A Nerd's Eye View ™

Cyber Security

for Seniors

Steve Krantz, Ph.D.

Cyber Security for Seniors

ISBN: 9781794698055

Imprint: Independently published

Trademarks

All terms mentioned in this book that are known to be trademarks or service marks have been appropriately capitalized. Alan Steven Krantz cannot attest to the accuracy of this information. Use of a term in this book should not be regarded as affecting the validity of any trademark or service mark.

Warning and Disclaimer

Every effort has been made to make this book as complete and as accurate as possible, but no warranty or fitness is implied. The information provided is on an "as is" basis. The author and publisher, Alan Steven Krantz, shall have neither liability nor responsibility to any person or entity with respect to any loss or damages arising from the information contained in this book.

Table of Contents

Table of Figures

Cyber Security for Seniors

Acknowledgements

Thanks to my son Jeffrey Krantz for inspiring the course that led to this book. His shared insights and experiences as a computer service expert were invaluable.

My son Paul Krantz, an attorney, provided valuable legal and aesthetic insight.

Thanks to my nephew Robert Michlowitz for his expert suggestions for content.

I am grateful to Jim Hoskins, CEO of Cogability™, for his friendship and wise counsel.

My friend, Warren S. Reid, distinguished computer expert, international IT expert witness, author, educator, and consultant, provided wonderful suggestions to improve usability and completeness.

I will always be grateful to my beautiful wife Annick for her care and being a sounding board for improvements to the text.

Author Biography

Dr. Steve Krantz retired from a 39 year career at IBM® in 2007 as a Distinguished Engineer. He holds a Ph.D. in Computer Science from Nova Southeastern University (1995). For the last 8 years of his IBM career, he was Chief Architect and Strategy Leader of IBM's worldwide, internal IT infrastructure, responsible for the successful computing support of over 400,000 professionals, technicians and administrators.

Steve is a member of the Board of PFLAG Los Angeles and a member of the Board of The Lavender Effect, local organizations dedicated to the civil rights of LGBTQ persons. He served as Director of PFLAG's Southern Pacific Region and as a member of PFLAG's National Board from 2007 through 2013.

He was a long distance runner for over 30 years, having completed the New York Marathon twice and the LA Marathon 3 times. For the past ten years, he has attempted a second sports career as a tennis player!

With his late wife Joan, Steve is the parent of two adult sons, Jeff and Paul. With his wife Annick, he is step-dad to her two adult children, Amanda and Eric. Annick and Steve live happily in the San Fernando Valley of Los Angeles.

A. Introduction

The audience for this book are seniors who are active Internet users through their computers or smartphones or tablets, who want to minimize the risks of today's cyber environment. It is sensible to be fearful of these risks, while at the same time eager for the benefits. Hopefully, the book will provide a guide to self-protection for all readers.

I start with B. Security Checklist that links to the Do's and Don'ts throughout the book. Use it as a guide to keep all of your online activities and electronic devices secure even after you finish reading this book.

Next is a simple definition of cyber security. Given this definition, we discuss the risks we face from the threat of cybercrimes, such as watering hole attacks, phishing and other scams.

With this groundwork laid, we lightly cover the common technology tools that underpin our personal cyber experiences with smartphones, tablets, laptops and the like. The bulk of the book will step through each of the protections – i.e. the solutions and practices - developed to avoid or defeat the risks.

Kindle vs. Print Version Note: There are many "hot" links in the book, from footnotes with Web addresses to internal page # links. The Kindle version will preserve this interactivity for those who want to go deeper into my research references and use the Security Checklist in a dynamic fashion. The Print version will include the links, but require more traditional follow-up.

B. Security Checklist

The following table is a list of the most important **security recommendations** (do's, don'ts, nevers, etc.) in the book. *I believe that if you take these "steps," your online life will be much more secure and you will realize the true value of your investment in this book.*

(Over time, it is likely that these steps will change with the changing security landscape. To keep up, refer to my website, www.nerdsiview.com, where a current, downloadable checklist is available.)

The table has 6 columns:

1. **#** - *Step* Number.
2. **Step** - Recommended Activity.
3. **Priority** of importance - H for high, M for medium, L for low but still important.
4. **Chapter** - chapter reference within the book.
5. **When** - when to do it.
6. **Done** - space for you, the reader, to keep track.

Security Checklist

#	Step	Prio rity	Chapter	When	Done?
1	Freeze your credit at the 4 credit bureaus and check credit rating annually at each.	H	Q. Financial	Once then Yearly	
2	Create long, memorable passwords at all online accounts.	H	J. Passwords	Once	
3	Set up two-factor authentication (2FA) at your financial accounts (banking, investments, credit cards).	H	J.2. Two Factor Authenticati on (2FA)	Once	
4	Set up your home router with a non-personal SSID, memorable and strong password, WPA2 encryption, firewall enabled and remote management turned off. Consult a professional, if necessary (see V.1. Consulting a Professional).	H	F.2. A Secure Home Router is a Must	Once	
5	In email, don't click on attachments or links unless SURE of source.	H	M. Email & Snail Mail	When-ever	
6	Keep software (operating system, web browser…) up to date on all devices using only the native auto-update feature.	H	O. Personal Computers	When-ever	

Cyber Security for Seniors
B. Security Checklist

#	Step	Priority	Chapter	When	Done?
7	Install antivirus on personal computer(s) and smartphone(s).	H	I. Antivirus Software	Once	
8	Maintain a remote backup of personal computer and smartphone files.	H	R.2. Backup/Recovery	Once	
9	If virus-infected, run antivirus or consult a professional (V.1. Consulting a Professional).	H	D.7. Are You a Victim?	Whenever	
10	Change all passwords when a major breach occurs.	H	D.6. Major Data Breach?	Whenever	
11	Create Kick the Bucket letter for your heirs.	H	S. Kicking the Bucket	Once	
12	Use Public Wi-Fi only with a secure VPN. Avoid online financial transactions on public Wi-Fi.	H	G. Networks	Whenever	
13	Setup a software firewall on personal devices through operating system or security suite.	H	H. Firewalls	Once	
14	Don't send important personal information, in text messages	M	N. Texting	Whenever	
15	Minimize sharing of your cell phone number.	M	J.3. Minimize Sharing Your Phone Number	Whenever	

Cyber Security for Seniors
B. Security Checklist

#	Step	Prio rity	Chapter	When	Done?
16	If email is important, upgrade to business service for nominal cost.	M	M.1. Consider Paying for Your Email Service	Once	
17	Check your personal exposure on the Dark Web at https://haveibeenpwned.com	M	D.3. The Dark Web	When-ever	
18	Avoid entering online contests/surveys, mailing in warranty cards, excessive posting on Social Media.	M	L. Social Media	When-ever	
19	If scam victim, change passwords, run antivirus, call police, contact credit bureaus, financial companies.	M	D.7. Are You a Victim?	When-ever	
20	Create a smartphone lock screen with alternate phone number and email.	M	P.1. Physical Device Security	When-ever	
21	Only use your own cable connected to a traditional (120V) plug if charging device in a public place	M	E.4. Technology and Security	When-ever	
22	Login to your home router to perform needed maintenance (e.g. update firmware) annually. Consult a professional if necessary (V.1. Consulting a Professional).	M	F.2. A Secure Home Router is a Must	Yearly	

#	Step	Priority	Chapter	When	Done?
23	Install a Password Manager and delete all passwords from your browser.	M	J.1. Password Managers	Once	
24	When web browsing to a new site, examine the address bar details to ensure security.	M	K. Web Browsing	When-ever	
25	Encrypt your files on all devices. Consult a professional, if necessary (see V.1. Consulting a Professional).	M	O.2. Disk (Storage) Encryption	Once	
26	When migrating to a new computer or smartphone, carefully erase all files. Consult a professional, if necessary (see V.1. Consulting a Professional).	M	O.3. How do I securely dispose of my old personal computer?, P.7. Migrate from Old to New Smartphone (Securely)	When-ever	
27	Use touch/facial recognition (if available) and a non-obvious pass code for all devices.	M	P.1. Physical Device Security	Once	
28	Minimize use of location and contact sharing.	M	P.2. Location Sharing, P.3. Contact Sharing	Once	

Cyber Security for Seniors
B. Security Checklist

#	Step	Prio rity	Chapter	When	Done?
29	Set up a pin access code with your phone service provider.	M	P.4. Telephone Account Access	Once	
30	Turn off your "local" communications features (e.g. Bluetooth, AirDrop, network sharing) when in public places.	L	E.4. Technology and Security	When-ever	
31	Minimize tracking of your browser activity by going incognito or installing a blocking extension.	L	K.1. Minimizing Online Ads	When-ever	
32	Establish accounts at major, official websites before a scammer does it for you.	L	K.2. Shoppers Beware	Once	
33	Stick with known stores when shopping online.	L	K.2. Shoppers Beware	When-ever	
34	Clean up stale website personal data.	L	K.3. Clean Up Stale Digital Haunts and Personal Data	Yearly	
35	Review sharing and privacy settings for all social media accounts.	L	L. Social Media	Once	
36	Reduce stored emails.	L	M.2. Reduce Stored Emails	Yearly	
37	Set your devices to lock after a short time of inactivity.	L	O.1. Physical Access Control	Once	

14

Cyber Security for Seniors

#	Step	Priority	Chapter	When	Done?
38	For excessive robo calls, contact phone service providers for blocking services.	L	P.6. Guidance to Minimize Vishing (Spam Calls)	Once	
39	If smished, forward the message to 7726 to report it.	L	N.1. Have You Been Smished?	When-ever	
40	Frequently monitor financial accounts and set up automatic alerts.	L	Q. Financial	Daily	
41	Use smartphone "Pay" apps for more secure payments.	L	Q.3. Making Payments Securely in the 21st Century	When-ever	
42	Purge unnecessary files on all devices periodically.	L	R.1. What to Keep and How Long to Keep It?	Yearly	

C. What is Cyber Security

In *1968*, a prescient political scientist wrote the following[1]: "By 2018 it will be cheaper to store information in a computer … than on paper." "Tax returns, social security records, census forms, military records, perhaps a criminal record, hospital records, security clearance files, school transcripts…bank statements, credit ratings, job records," and more would be stored on computers that could communicate worldwide. "By 2018 the *researcher* sitting at his console will be able to compile a cross-tabulation of consumer purchases (from store records) by people of low IQ (from school records) who have an unemployed member of the family (from social security records). That is, he will have the technological capability to do this. Will he have the legal right?" Clearly, this was a stunningly accurate prediction of today's state of affairs, although sadly, the *researcher* today is too often a criminal.

Fast forward to 2017 when a Pew Research survey determined that half of Americans do not trust modern institutions to protect their personal data. Ironically, those same Americans "frequently neglect cyber security best practices in their own personal lives." This is despite the fact that "a majority of Americans (64%) have personally experienced a major data breach" and "58% of Americans age 50 and older are especially likely to feel that their personal information has become less safe in recent years." [2]

---

[1] Ithiel de Sola Pool, Foreign Policy Association, *Toward the Year 2018*, Cowles Education Corp., 1968.
[2] Pew Research Survey - January, 2017

Cyber security is the protection of Internet-connected systems, including hardware, software and data, from cyberattacks and physical loss.

Cyber Security Goals are:

- No loss of personal data or computing devices.
- No loss of privacy for all personal data.
- Operate securely everywhere: home, work, airports, etc.

C.1. What is your personal risk?

Here's a personal exposure *test* that will help you measure your risk. Total the numbers of your answers and compare it to the descriptions in the *Scoring* section at the end to determine your exposure to negative consequences:

- The information you post online is:

  1. Next to nothing
  2. Only the most basic information
  3. Professional & business data only
  4. Personal
  5. Everything I think or do

- Do you publish a blog?
  1. No
  2. Yes, but it can only be accessed by small group of close friends

3. Yes, but it can only be accessed by small group of friends, some of whom I have not met personally
4. Yes, it's a public blog, but I never write about my personal life
5. Yes, I write about myself for everyone to see

- How often do you post on Facebook?
  1. Never.
  2. Less than once a month
  3. At least weekly
  4. Daily
  5. Many times a day
- Your personal Web presence can be described as:
  1. A few words of text
  2. Anonymous reviews and comments
  3. A short personal biography
  4. Biography, pictures and videos
  5. All of the above, plus postings
  6. I post naked pictures of myself online

- Scoring
  - o   4-7 - Careful and protective
  - o   8-11 - Just testing the waters
  - o   12-16 - Unabashed Internet junkie
  - o   17-21 - Baring everything[3]

Reading this book is mandatory if you are an 8 or more! Your author is a 12 – ouch!!!

---

[3] Protecting Your Internet Identity, Claypoole and Payton, Rowman & Littlefield, 2017

Your personal risk is also a function of how much of your personal and family's information is stored in online storage and accessible by others. Unless this information is properly protected, such as by encryption, it is liable to expose you to fraud, extortion and embarrassment. Ask yourself the following questions:

- What's online about you and your family?
  - Social Media accounts?
  - Physical residence information?
  - Vacation planning?
  - Financial records?
- What is your exposure to fraud, extortion, embarrassment?
  - Financial loss?
  - Family matters exposed?
  - Political and charitable giving exposed?

Beyond online information exposure, the number of devices and users that operate in your home may add additional risk. Care needs to be taken when cyber devices are shared among users of different practices and skill, for example among grandparents, parents and their children.

So, reflect on the following:

- How many personal computers, mobile devices, tablets, TVs, home security systems, and appliances are connected to your home Wi-Fi network?
  - Are they shared across personal and home office use?
  - What backup procedures are in place for each device?
- Do non-family members regularly in your home have access to your Wi-Fi network or computing devices?

- Are you or other household members active on social media like Facebook, Twitter, Instagram or other social media apps?

After reflecting on your personal exposure, we turn now to how the "bad guys" have and will exploit it.

D. Cybercrimes

D.1. Everyone's Getting Hacked

Major corporations are getting hacked. The Marriott breach in 2018 was said to be part of a Chinese intelligence effort that also breached health insurers and security clearance databases. Up to 500 million customers may have been affected in this breach, one of the largest breaches in history. [4]

Figure 1 - Everyone's Getting Hacked

---

[4] NY Times, December 11, 2018

Media organizations are getting hacked, such as Sony in 2014 by the North Koreans. Tech companies are getting hacked, such as Adobe in 2013 and Facebook in 2018.

The Equifax breach in 2017 was especially troubling as Equifax is one of the four major guardians of our personal credit ratings (Experian, Transunion and Innovis are the other three). Congress is considering legislation in 2019 to subject "credit-reporting companies to tougher cybersecurity standards and making it easier for consumers to fix errors on their credit reports" [5] as a result. It was announced in July 2019 that a settlement was reached to compensate victims[6].

Critical infrastructure is getting hacked, such as the US electrical grid by the Russians in 2016-2018[7]. The hackers used a *watering hole attack* – planting malicious code in familiar websites – to lure unsuspecting Federal contractors to reveal personal information, ultimately allowing them to secure access to critical US electrical grid infrastructure.

"Dating" websites are getting hacked. Small companies are getting hacked. National political parties are getting hacked, such as the Democratic Party in 2016.

Everybody and their grandparents are getting hacked these days – that means *US*, fellow senior citizens!

---

[5] Wall Street Journal, January 2, 2019
[6] https://www.ftc.gov/enforcement/cases-proceedings/refunds/equifax-data-breach-settlement .
[7] https://www.wsj.com/articles/americas-electric-grid-has-a-vulnerable-back-doorand-russia-walked-through-it-11547137112?

D.2. Everyone's Reality

"If someone wants to find my social security number (SSN), it will take them exactly $3 and five minutes", as recently noted in the Wall Street Journal. [8] This is a startling revelation for us seniors, as we have guarded our SSN most of our lives. We have long thought that it is a key to our personal histories – educational, work, medical, etc. To realize now that some jerk can masquerade as us using our SSN forces us to take the concrete measures I describe in this book; for example, freezing our credit (to be detailed later).

Reality #1: Bad guys already have access to your personal data based on the number and scope of nationwide security breaches.

- Credit card information, Social Security number, mother's maiden name, date of birth, address, previous addresses, smartphone number, and credit file may already be available for sale on the Dark Web (see next section).

Reality #2: Any data shared with a company will in all likelihood eventually be hacked, lost, leaked, stolen or sold.

- Usually through no fault of your own.
- As an American, your recourse is limited or nil!!

---

[8] Wall Street Journal, December 10, 2018

D.3. The Dark Web

It's sad, but the *Dark Web* offers our personal data for sale to bad guys worldwide. "The dark web is the World Wide Web content that exists on darknets, overlay networks that use the Internet but require specific software, configurations, or authorization to access." [9]

When a major company gets hacked, where does the stolen personal information end up? Many times, it is up for sale on the Dark Web. In Figure 2, you see a screenshot - the result of a search for illegal goods on a Dark Web website. Your "normal" web search tools, such as Google search, won't find this website. To get there, you use the *TOR* browser, which is specially designed to hide the searcher's identity. Also designed to protect the searcher's privacy is the DuckDuckGo search engine, which is then used to find the website. It is shocking to see the wares for sale – drugs, forgeries, weapons, counterfeits. It is as commercial as any of our legitimate markets, with ratings, disclaimers and comments as would be found on Amazon.

---

[9] Wikipedia.org – "Dark Web"

Cyber Security for Seniors
D. Cybercrimes

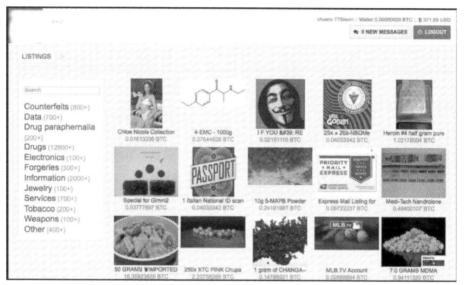

Figure 2 - Dark Web Products for Sale

To check your personal exposure to prominence on the Dark Web in an objective way, check Microsoft's Troy Hunt's https://haveibeenpwned.com[10]. The term "pwned" is computer gamer slang for "owned" or "totally defeated." You may sadly discover how many times your personal email address is listed in the Dark Web.

An alternate approach to checking your exposure, if you use Chrome as your web browser, is to install Google's Password Checkup extension. [11] When you login to a website, it'll check to see if your ID and password have been previously leaked in a data breach. Changing your password is then mandatory – more about passwords in chapter J. Passwords.

---

[10] https://en.wikipedia.org/wiki/Troy_Hunt
[11] https://lifehacker.com/how-to-make-sure-your-passwords-havent-been-stolen-1837305758?

D.4. Cybercrime Actors

In the table below, we list an assortment of malware types intended to defraud unsuspecting victims. Some are pure technology, such as a keylogger. Some are combinations of simple acts coupled with deception, such as a phishing email. Later you will see examples of this, some remarkably clever.

Assorted Malware Types

Malware Type	Description
Keylogger	A technology that records consecutive keystrokes on a keyboard to capture username and password information.
Phishing	An email, imitating a legitimate organization, sent to a user to obtain financial or other confidential information for malicious purposes.
Spear Phishing	A highly personal form of phishing that appears to come from a friend or financial institution.
Whaling	A type of spear phishing that targets a high value individual.
Vishing	A voice call, falsely representing a legitimate organization, seeking personal information for malicious intent.
Smishing	A text, falsely representing a legitimate organization, seeking personal information for malicious intent.

Cyber Security for Seniors
D. Cybercrimes

Malware Type	Description
Ransomware	A type of malware that restricts access to the files on a personal computer system until the user pays a ransom to the criminals.
Watering Hole Attack	A type of malware that is placed on a trusted website to surreptitiously collect personal information for malicious intent.

Although the actual criminal act can take several forms, the basic steps are often similar. **Figure 3**, below, illustrates a relatively common phishing scenario:

Step 1: The thief sends an email with a link or attachment to the victim that appears to come from a known party. The targeted victim then clicks the link or attachment, which includes malicious software (malware) that infects the victim's personal computer.

Step 2: The virus (the installed malware) steals login credentials to the victim's financial accounts.

Step 3: The virus transmits the stolen credentials to the thief.

Step 4: The thief, masquerading as the victim, logs in to the financial website.

Step 5: The thief transfers the victim's money to his account.

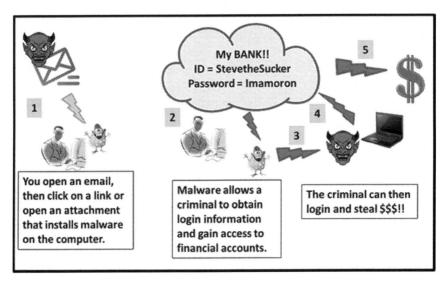

Figure 3 - The Makings of a Cybercrime

D.5. Scams

The following figure is an example of a "Blue Screen of Death" pop-up, which can appear when an unwitting user clicks on a scammer's link or opens a bogus attachment. It's a false offer of technical support intended to trick the victim into allowing remote access to their personal computer.

Sometimes, telephone calls (cold calls) to unsuspecting users is employed. Such tricks are mostly targeted at Microsoft® Windows® users, with the pop-up or caller claiming to represent a Microsoft technical support department. Customer support NEVER calls unless they are called first, so this should be recognized as an obvious scam.

Cyber Security for Seniors
D. Cybercrimes

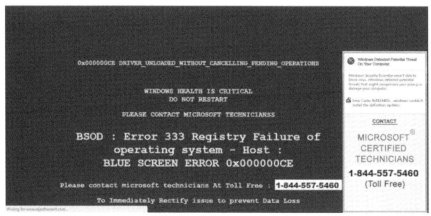

Figure 4 - Blue Screen of Death

Figure 5, below, is a pop-up ad, typically generated by going to a scammer's website, presenting a "too good to be true" opportunity which should be immediately ignored.

Figure 5 - Too Good to be True Pop-up Ad

The last example, below, is a sophisticated phishing email which I have personally received. I was stunned to see a personal password included in the spam. It attempted to extort money in exchange for not revealing personally embarrassing information to friends and family. After recovering from my shock, I used Google search to check if this was a known phishing scam – and it was. I immediately changed the offending password on the site I had previously used it. I also breathed a sigh of relief that I didn't succumb to its threat and pay off this criminal!

Finally, I took note of the video/audio eavesdropping threat at the end, and recommend that all of us **put tape over the video camera and microphone on our personal computers**.

Abcdefgh is one of your personal passwords and now I will cut to the chase. You don't know anything about me however I know you and you must be wondering why you are getting this mail, right?
I installed malware on adult vids (pornography) and guess what, you visited same sex web site to have pleasure (if you know what I mean). When you were watching videos, your device started out operating as a RDP (Remote Desktop Protocol) with a backdoor which gave me access to your display and your webcam controls. Immediately after that, the malware collected all your contacts from your messenger, fb, as well as e-mail.
I ... made a double-screen video to send to your contacts. First half displays the recording you were watching and next part shows the video of your web camera (it is you doing inappropriate things). I will give you two options which will make it happen. These two choices are to either turn a blind eye to this e mail (not recommended), or pay me 0.8 BTC. Notice: You now have one day to make the payment.

Figure 6 - Personal Information Phishing Scam

The AARP advises of **activities to avoid** that can lead online scammers to you:

- Entering online contests.
- Mailing in warranty cards.
- Filling out lots of online surveys.
- Posting lots of personal information on Social Media (more on this in section L. Social Media).

AARP further notes that much personal data is simply a consequence of living in the United States. Many public records are available at all government levels: census data, property information, criminal records, and bankruptcies. Private companies can legally gather this information and sell it.

For ongoing information on current scams that affect seniors, check the AARP's helpful website https://www.aarp.org/money/scams-fraud/ . [12]

D.6. Major Data Breach?

It has become an all-too-frequent occurrence – a highly visible, important corporation or organization has been hacked, revealing the personal information of millions. So what to do?

- **Check for Potential Impact(s)** – Major organizations whose data has been breached nearly always set up a website for their clients to check if they are affected. Many states require that individuals be contacted by mail if they are a part of a major breach. You may get a state-mandated letter and even if you don't, check for impact immediately.

---

[12] https://www.aarp.org/money/scams-fraud/

- **Use Offer of Free Credit Monitoring** – Enroll as soon as possible. It doesn't prevent identity theft but does provide alerts for any other later impacts, should they occur.
- **Change your Passwords and Logins immediately** – Do this for all accounts that might be affected. Consider adding two-factor authentication (see J.2. Two Factor Authentication (2FA)) while you are in this process.[13]

---

[13] https://cybercrimesupport.org/six-steps-to-take-immediately-after-learning-of-a-data-breach/

D.7. Are You a Victim?

If you are unlucky enough to be a victim of cybercrime, don't hesitate to take action. *Specific advice for preventing and/or resolving the various cybercrimes and associated risks are the essence of this text and will be presented in later sections.* In general, you should:

- Change your passwords on your personal computer and any password-protected websites you visit (especially financial institutions).
- If you have protective software, such as antivirus software, run a full scan immediately.
- Call your local police department or district attorney's office and, if needed, the FBI and the Federal Trade Commission (FTC).
- If you believe that your personal identity has been stolen - for example, that someone can gain credit in your name or can steal from your online-accessible accounts - it's time to contact the four main credit bureaus, your bank and investment companies.
- Check out the Cybercrime Support Network at www.fraudsupport.org. Founded in 2017, it offers support for cybercrime victims.
- Regarding the Equifax breach, mentioned earlier, victims can seek financial restitution as the result of a settlement. [14]

---

[14] https://www.ftc.gov/enforcement/cases-proceedings/refunds/equifax-data-breach-settlement

Cyber Security for Seniors
D. Cybercrimes

Now that you better understand your risks in the cyber world, we turn to an explanation of the technologies and its infrastructure that we use on a daily basis. I hope it will be a confidence builder.

E. Technology Basics

E.1. How the Internet Works in a Nutshell

Refer to the figure below to follow the flow. The numbers in the following bullets correspond to the numbers in the figure.

1. From your laptop, you open your Web browser and try to connect to a website, let's call it www.xyz.com . At this point, your personal computer sends an electronic *request* through your home router, then through your modem, over your Internet connection to your Internet Service Provider's (ISP) server which will ultimately send the *request* to a Domain Name Server or DNS.

2. The DNS server will look for a match for the domain name you've typed in (www.xyz.com). If it finds a match, it will translate www.xyz.com into the associated address based on the Internet Protocol, or IP. In this fictional case, it is 3.454.65.

3. The DNS then sends this address to an IP *router* which finds the Web server that corresponds to 3.454.65 and routes the *request* to it.

4. The server at IP address 3.454.65 has the webpages that comprise the website www.xyz.com . The www.xyz.com server then will respond by sending the requested webpage back to your laptop as a series of packets. Each packet is a small part of the webpage – between 1000 and 1500 characters (or bytes). Packets also have information that tell servers on the network and your laptop their origin address, target address and re-assembly instructions back into a webpage. When the packets get to your

laptop, it arranges them according to the rules of the protocols used, such as https.

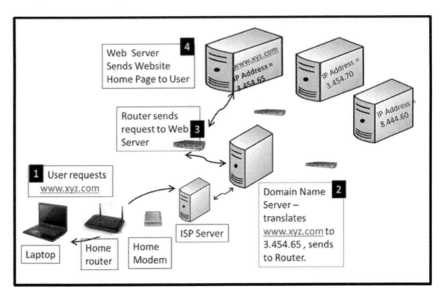

Figure 7 - How the Internet Works

E.2. Technology "Heritage" (Tongue in Cheek)

In the beginning, there was the Apple 1 which begat the IBM PC, and the IBM PC begat the IBM ThinkPad and the Compaq and the Dell, and, and, and…..

And the Apple Newton begat the iPad and the Blackberry mated with the iPad to begat the iPhone which begat the HTC Dream (??) which begat the Android smartphone.

And Netscape Navigator begat Internet Explorer and Safari and Firefox and Chrome.

And so it goes………………..

E.3. Technology Terms

I hope that now you are in prayerful mood with all that "begatting" so that I can get serious and explain a bit of the terminology for purposes of understanding this book.

Following are the general technology terms that I will use in this book:

- **Smartphone** – we should all be familiar with the small, pocket-sized electronic device that provides wireless telephone calls, enables web browsing, event calendaring and other personal computing activities with a touchscreen interface.

- **Tablet** – an electronic device with the functions and interface of a smartphone, but with a larger screen size.

- **Personal Computer** – an electronic device for processing and storing data complete with a display and a keyboard. It is a general term for both laptop and desktop systems.

- **Laptop** – a portable, personal computer with the functions and size of a tablet and a keyboard interface. In some cases, a touchscreen interface is also provided.

- **Desktop** – a non-portable, personal computer.

- **Web Browser**- software that enables searching the World Wide Web on the Internet.

- **Operating System** – software that supports a computer's or smartphone's basic functions.

Figure 8 relates these general technology terms to the representative product of the most prominent manufacturers. I will refer to these throughout the book as appropriate.

The Operating System row includes Android® and Windows® operating systems which have been made available to additional device manufacturers for use in their products. For example, Samsung makes the Galaxy® line of smartphones with the Android operating system included and Lenovo makes the Thinkpad® line of laptops with the Windows operating system included. As a result, I will refer to any smartphone with the Android operating system as an "Android smartphone" and any personal computer with the Windows operating system as a "Windows computer".

Refer to section 'W. Glossary' for definitions of additional terms as needed.

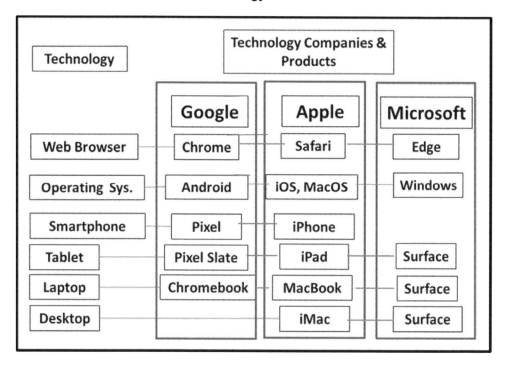

Figure 8 - Technology vs. Manufacturer

E.4. Technology and Security

As I developed this book, the nerd in me organized the solutions and practices that apply to cyber security. I realized that there are a set of natural security "categories" into which each such solution and/or practice fits: device, personal, operational, application, network and storage.

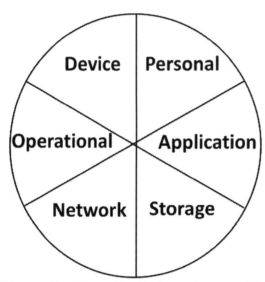

Figure 9 - Security Categories vs. Technology

- *Device Security* - the solutions/practices to protect a device (smartphone, tablet, laptop) from loss, to access (or open or unlock) it, to control how long it remains unlocked when idle and additional controls for parents (and in our case grandparents!). The protective solutions and practices include:
  - **Passwords, Pins** – character strings, phrases or number sequences required for user entry to gain access to a personal computer or smartphone.
  - **Lock Screen** – a visual image on a personal computer or smartphone screen that appears when the device is turned on or after a timeout.
  - **Timeout** - a set period of device idle time that triggers appearance of a lock screen.

- o **Software Device Recovery** - software and communications to track and facilitate the recovery of a lost or stolen device.

- o **Parental Control** – software tools that allow parents to control time constraints or off-limits websites for their children.

- *Personal Security* - securing your person and your personal contacts. Being personally secure in the cyber security context implies controlling who or what cyber entity is aware of your personal information, your location and your social contacts. You control this through application or operating system or device settings to allow or deny such information sharing.

- *Operational Security* - aims to ensure sound device functioning through active measures, such anti-virus software, operating system software updates and tune-up actions such as file storage cleanup.

- *Application Security* - includes passwords and enhanced authentication methods (e.g. two-factor authentication) for application/website access, software updates to correct vulnerabilities and recognition of annoying or criminal communications in email, or spam.

- *Network Security* – includes special hardware and software to monitor data traffic to prevent unwanted intrusion, such as firewalls, and encrypt transmissions to protect privacy.

- **Storage Security** – software methods to protect stored information (data file) theft through encryption and information loss through backup processes.

The figure below illustrates how the technology items connect us at home, in the outside world and how the cyber security protections apply.

E.5. The Home Environment

For many of us, most of our personal computer activities occur at home. At the bottom of the figure, we see the commonplace communication between our laptop personal computer sending and receiving data on our Wi-Fi network at home. For security purposes, we have selected a non-personal Wi-Fi network name (SSID) and provided a STRONG associated password (more later in chapter J. Passwords). Encrypted data goes from our laptop to our router to our modem device, which then transmits it through the Internet to its ultimate Internet-based server. The next step is typically a return data flow from the server, such as a web page, filtered through the firewalls in our router and our network software to ensure it is coming from our intended source. A similar interaction occurs if we are using our smartphone at home for Internet access via Wi-Fi.

E.6. The Outside World

The top half of **Figure 10** represents the outside world, where there is more variety of communication. Our smartphones and tablets can use the cellular data network, traditionally used for voice communication, to communicate to and from the Internet. This data stream uses encryption to protect it from eavesdroppers. Our smartphones and laptops have the option of using public Wi-Fi to and from the Internet, which is much riskier than either cellular or Wi-Fi from home, as it is unencrypted. A more secure approach is to use a Virtual Private Network or VPN, which only sends encrypted data through the network, over the Public Wi-Fi.

There is yet another risk of operating your device in a public place, even if you are using a VPN – your "local area" communication options - include file/printer sharing, Bluetooth, and AirDrop. When in public, turn them off! While on, any nearby scammers can gain access to your device and do damage.

- On a Windows computer, go to Settings → Network and Internet → Sharing Options → turn off file and printer sharing.
- For Macs, go to System Preferences, then Sharing, and unselect everything. Then head to Finder → AirDrop → select Allow me to be discovered by: No One.
- For your iPhone or iPad, go to Settings → General → AirDrop → Receiving Off.

Sad to say, even charging your device in a public place, such as the airport, is risky today. Public USB charging stations can be hacked by scammers to put malware on your device. And don't use a casually discarded charging cable – it too may have been modified to deliver malware. Only use your own cable connected to a traditional (120V) plug if charging in a public place. A final point on the figure is that you may not have a modem and router as separate physical devices at home, it might instead be a combination modem/router provided by your Internet service provider (your ISP).

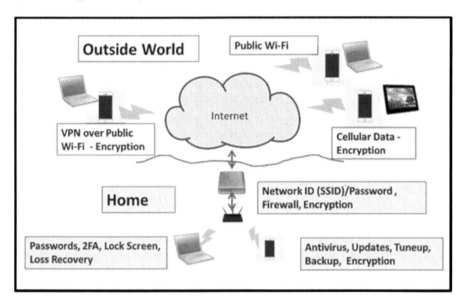

Figure 10 - Technology Connections to Security

This section, "E.Technology Basics", illustrated the typical devices and their relationships with the cyber world. We introduced the general approaches to security and protections. Now we will go into more depth focusing on:

- The major protections that apply across applications, operating systems and devices, such as passwords and antivirus software.
- The major applications that we use, such as email and browsing, and their applicable protections.

Cyber Security for Seniors
E. Technology Basics

- Our devices such as personal computers and smartphones, and their applicable protections.
- Our stored files for recordkeeping, reference and recreation, such as tax files, photos and music, and the methods to protect them.

Protections are either actions you can take or products or services you can acquire that will prevent, avoid or remedy negative events in your cyber experience. We start with the typically one-time experience of setting up your home network router.

F. Routers

F.1. A Cautionary Tale

My son the computer guru, whose business is to service locals, was visiting one of his customer's residences to remove a particularly nasty computer virus. He discovered that the likely source of the virus was an insecure home router - the customer's router administrator password was "*password*"!

F.2. A Secure Home Router is a Must

The wireless router in your home network needs one-time setup as a device, with an access ID and password for the administrator (usually you!). When this is complete, the administrator (you) sets up your home network.

This one-time effort should be done carefully – see **Figure 11**. Choose a unique, memorable router ID and STRONG, memorable password (more later on this) to administer the router's settings.

Next, following your router's instructions, **set up your home network by creating a unique, memorable network name** – also called an SSID – that offers NO personal or familial reference. This name is broadcast in your neighborhood, so it shouldn't identify your family or home. You should also **create a STRONG, memorable password to be used by each home-based device when seeking Wi-Fi access**.

At the same time, you will **select a data encryption option for the Wi-Fi network – WPA2** should be selected, unless WPA3 is available. **Wi**-Fi **P**rotected **A**ccess (**WPA**) are data encryption standards for users of computing devices equipped with wireless Internet connections.   Both offer superior data encryption to the original data encryption option, WEP.

Next, ensure that your router's **firewall is enabled** to protect your Wi-FI network from unwanted incoming data traffic.

Figure 11 - Home Router Setup

Finally, some routers allow *remote access* to a router's controls, enabling the manufacturer to provide technical support, as an option. Some routers support the UPnP home networking protocol which supports remote access for gamers.   **Never leave these remote management features enabled**. Hackers can use them to get into your home network.

Cyber Security for Seniors
F. Routers

While the network setup is a one-time activity, as the router administrator, you should plan on an annual login to perform any needed maintenance; e.g. updating the router's firmware from the router manufacturer's website. If unsure how to do this, as it's a very occasional and very important activity, consult a professional (see V.1. Consulting a Professional).

G. Networks

As mentioned earlier, regarding technology basics, your home Wi-Fi network is secure if properly set up (e.g. hardware firewall should be enabled and WPA2 data encryption selected).

When away from home, there are two primary choices: connecting your smartphone or laptop to public Wi-Fi - as is commonly available in an airport, an AirBnb or, for example, a Starbucks™ restaurant - or using your smartphone's cellular data capability.

- **Public Wi-Fi is insecure**, even with password access, and should never be used for financial transactions, unless a Virtual Private Network (VPN) service can be employed (see discussion below).

- **Cellular data transmission is generally considered to be secure**. On a typical 4G (4th Generation as supplied by vendors like AT&T® or Verizon®) cellular network connection, data is encrypted and the user's identity is authenticated and protected.

G.1. Virtual Private Networks

A Virtual Private Network (VPN) is a service that supports data encryption and uses a server that reroutes the user's Internet activities. VPNs protect and secure a user's identity and information. If you travel frequently, use public Wi-Fi services or have serious security concerns about your home network, you can purchase VPN service from several quality vendors[15]. Check out the trial period when making your selection – longest is best. [16]

If you believe that you are the target of a serious Internet criminal, investment in a VPN may be warranted to allow your activities to be truly private on the Internet. [17]

Note that a VPN, whether on your personal computer or smartphone, ONLY protects (encrypts, re-routes) your web browsing, social media and email activities over the Internet. Voice calls and texting operate on the cellular data network, separate from the Internet – see chapter V.2. Data Transmission & Storage Security for an overview.

G.2. Privacy Controls with ISP

Be sure to exercise any privacy controls offered by your Internet Service Provider (ISP). They are the first stop in the pipeline of your Internet usage, the first stop in reducing your personal exposure. In addition to personal enrollment data, they are able to track all your usage. **Opt for minimal sharing with third parties**, such as their affiliates, government (state, Federal), etc.

---

[15] https://www.cnet.com/best-vpn-services-directory/
[16] https://www.zdnet.com/article/how-to-choose-the-vpn-thats-right-for-you/?
[17] For example, you are a public official, wealthy and/or famous person.

H. Firewalls

A firewall is "a piece of hardware or software that helps prevent malware and malicious attacks from entering a computer or a network of computers through the Internet." [18] It is a barrier that complements other security elements, such as antivirus software.

Hardware firewalls filter [judge] Internet data traffic, examining incoming data and filter it for its source and content, accepting incoming traffic from approved sources, denying incoming traffic from unapproved others. Most Internet routers have a built in firewall, thereby protecting all the devices connected to them. They are easy to set-up and connect to.

For monitoring outbound data traffic from your personal computer (or any single device), a software firewall is typically used. If a virus manages to elude the hardware firewall and installs itself on one of your devices, the software firewall should be able to trap any resultant problematic outbound data transmissions (e.g. a personal computer bot which broadcasts data from your device to harm other networked devices). Software firewalls are customizable to adjust to user needs (e.g. Internet gaming). They are available on most major operating systems and should be set up and used. If you invest in an add-on security suite, such as Norton™ 360, firewall software is typically included.

---

[18] Firewalls, https://www.wikipedia.org/

I. Antivirus Software

Antivirus software periodically checks device memory and files for dangerous, foreign code or files (small bits of software) and removes or nullifies its ability to affect your personal computer/smartphone's operation. Its function complements that of firewall filters, if and when malware slips through. It is an available component with most major operating systems and add-on security suites, such as Norton™ 360.

It offers clear benefits to personal computers running the Windows® operating system. However, antivirus software may be unnecessary for Mac®, iOS® (iPhone®) and Android® devices given their more secure operating system design and application deployment controls. Nevertheless, **antivirus software should be activated on all devices** when it is available.

J. Passwords

Passwords have been with us for millennia in many contexts – from military sentry challenges to today's cyber needs.

Based on Wikipedia[19], personal computers have always been adept at character-by-character entry, comparison and, too often, rejection! Guidance on password creation and oversight has varied over the years. It became more of a concern with the Internet and the advent of hacking. "Making good password choices is the single biggest control consumers have over their own personal security posture, " per security expert Troy Hunt. [20]

Previous password orthodoxy dictated a character assortment – letters of mixed case, numbers and special characters – of an 8-16 character length. This approach has recently been superseded by recommendations from the National Institute of Science and Technology to **create long, _memorable_ passwords**[21], such as "My cat Felicia eats fish for dinner." A clever combination of a long, memorable password phrase, but limited length, is to use the first letters of the phrase's words with a number and/or special character at the end, as a memorable compromise; e.g. McFeffd2# would be the memorable but shortened version of the phrase above.

It is further recommended **not to use the same passwords for any of your accounts**. This makes it harder for criminals to steal

---

[19] https://en.wikipedia.org/wiki/Password
[20] https://www.zdnet.com/article/these-are-the-most-commonly-hacked-passwords-and-theyre-embarrassingly-weak/?
[21] https://www.nist.gov/

access to your accounts and limit the damage they can do if they crack your code.

After selecting a password, use a password checker to gauge its strength, e.g. http://www.passwordmeter.com/. Some sites and applications restrict password length, so go back to the previous diverse-character guidance in these cases.

Change passwords when a major breach occurs, not on any regular schedule. Again, diversity across your online accounts should be standard practice.

As we know, every year there are data breaches and more sets of credentials (user IDs and passwords) are leaked onto the Internet. Criminals commonly collect these credential dumps and try these user IDs and passwords at financial sites, email providers, mobile smartphone providers, social media sites and others.

So, be especially careful with passwords for your financial accounts, making them long (as possible), memorable and diverse. Additional considerations for these accounts will be discussed later.

The value of enhanced checking at password entry is now recognized, in a recent study by the password manager company Dashlane.[22] It ranks popular websites on their password security policies. Dashlane's criteria include additional important security functions:

---

[22] https://blog.dashlane.com/dashlane-password-power-rankings-2017/

- Dynamic (i.e. as you enter the characters) rating of password strength.
- Denial of service in the face of repeated, brute force login attempts.
- Two Factor Authentication (2FA, which we will discuss later).

These criteria should be a consideration when selecting among alternative applications and websites.

J.1. Password Managers

Password Managers are, typically, an add-on software service that gathers IDs and passwords as you enter them at websites and applications. Once captured, the service will automatically enter them when you return to the site or app. Additional features vary across the competitors, including password strength checking and automatic password generation.

Password Managers services are now widely recommended, including by AARP®, to improve security for those with multiple online accounts and applications.

Dashlane and LastPass are two of the best-reviewed password managers that can be installed your personal computer and/or smartphone. They both support common storage, evaluation and generation of all web-based passwords, thereby improving your online security.

If you invest in a password manager, consider an annual ID and password review coupled with updates to all accounts.

I use Norton™ 360 suite for password management as well as its more familiar features, such as antivirus. It captured all my IDs and passwords that I used on my laptop. When I installed it on my iPhone, it automatically transferred these IDs and passwords for more convenient and secure browsing.

After installing your password manager, remove any passwords that your Web browser may be storing (duplicatively now) for you – this will prevent a hacker from learning this information if your browser-related account is hacked (e.g. Google or Microsoft).

- In Chrome (or in the Chromium-based Edge browser), press Ctrl+Shift+Delete to open the Clear Browsing Data dialog box. Click the Advanced tab, choose All Time for the Time Range, select the Passwords And Other Sign-in Data option, and then click Clear Data.
- In Microsoft Edge, press Alt+X to open the Settings And More menu, then click Settings. Select the Privacy & Security tab and click Clear Browsing Data. Select Passwords and then click Clear.[23]

J.2. Two Factor Authentication (2FA)

Strong passwords are only an initial barrier to hackers seeking access to your information. A next step to improve protection beyond passwords is called two factor authentication or 2FA. **Figure 12** illustrates a step-by-step example of how it works:

---

[23] https://www.zdnet.com/article/protect-your-online-identity-now-fight-hackers-with-these-5-security-precautions/?

Cyber Security for Seniors
J. Passwords

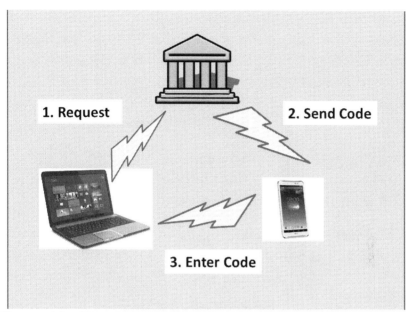

1. Request
2. Send Code
3. Enter Code

Figure 12 - Two-Factor Authentication

1. Login with ID and password (factor 1) to bank website from your personal computer.
2. Request transfer of funds to your investment account (for example).
3. Asked to enter numeric code to be sent to your smartphone (factor 2) before proceeding.
4. Text is sent to your smartphone containing numeric code.
5. You enter numeric code into entry field on your personal computer to PROVE it's you.
6. Transfer is made!

Always use two factor authentication (2FA), if available, when making changes to important online accounts.

To determine if your credit, banking and investment accounts offer 2FA, look in the app's or website's *Profile Settings*. They will typically offer sending texts or emails when account activity occurs or you make account changes. For example, Bank of America's *Profile Settings* includes a *Security Center* selection to set up 2FA.

Social media apps, such as Facebook, offer 2FA for additional security. If you authorize 2FA in your Facebook profile, it requires entry of a login code to ensure your personal identification.

There are also more general, software-based, 2FA services. They are apps that specifically deliver it in conjunction with many commercial websites, such as Authy, Duo Mobile and Google Authenticator.

A more secure, hardware-based, 2FA alternative for the truly security-concerned is the Yubikey, based on FIDO[24] (Fast IDentity Online) and U2F[25] standards. The key is a small device that plugs into a USB port in your personal computer. It interacts with many websites for secure 2FA identity verification.

Figure 13 - Yubikey

---

[24] https://fidoalliance.org/
[25] https://www.yubico.com/solutions/fido-u2f/

An example of another form of account activity notification, more reactive then preventative, is shown in **Figure 14**. We see an email from Netflix® – essentially an alert - about a possible third party logging in to the account.

Netflix Email
 New sign-in to Netflix
 Hi Steve,
 We noticed a new sign-in with your Netflix account (stevek@bipedinfo.com).
 Device , Computer ,
Location California, United States
(may not match your exact location)
Time
November 19th, 5:41 PM PST
 If you signed-in recently, relax and enjoy watching! But if you don't recognize this sign-in, we recommend that you change your password immediately to secure your account.
 We're here to help if you need it. Visit the Help Center for more info or contact us. –Your friends at Netflix

---

Figure 14 - 2FA Email from Netflix

In terms of most to least secure, the order of preference is:

1. Hardware key (such as the Yubikey),
2. A dedicated software 2FA app such as Authy or
3. Notification via text or email (per the 2FA example in **Figure 12**).

Again, take advantage of these features in your online accounts to maintain and improve your security. I am careful to indicate that

2FA *improves your security*, but practices 2 and 3 above can still be compromised by an enterprising hacker[26].

J.3. Minimize Sharing Your Phone Number

It comes down to the public availability of your cell phone number. It's very scary to realize that, with your cell phone number and the White Pages Premium web service, personal data is readily available, including current and past addresses, family names, other phone numbers (e.g. landlines) and property ownership information. [27]

So, what to do? Share your phone number very carefully. I only share my number as a basis for 2FA for web services I deem important, e.g. financial accounts, Consider setting up up a second phone number for people and services you don't entirely trust. Apps like Google Voice and Burner let you create a different number that you can use for calls and texts.

In the next section, Web Browsing, **Figure** 15 provides important additional clues to remaining safe online.

---

[26] https://www.nytimes.com/2019/01/27/opinion/2fa-cyberattacks-security.html?
[27] https://www.nytimes.com/2019/08/15/technology/personaltech/i-shared-my-phone-number-i-learned-i-shouldnt-have.html?searchResultPosition=1

K. Web Browsing

Your browser offers several clues to the safety and security of any website visit during a browsing session, as illustrated in **Figure 15**. Examine the browser's *address bar* to determine the website's relative security[28]:

- If there is a "lock" image, it implies relative security via an encrypted data link. If no lock image, it might specify (or imply) "not secure" or dangerous. Clicking on the lock will bring up a pop-up with details about the site's certification, including ownership and encryption status of the site's contents.
- If there is a company name after the lock, it means that the website has received "extended validation" or EV, providing stronger evidence of safety and security; essentially, the ownership of the website has been concretely identified through a trusted authority via the EV certificate. Even then, this identity verification just means that website belongs to the company it claims to belong to. It doesn't necessarily mean the company itself or its software is trustworthy.
- The https:// in front of the website address implies encrypted, secure transmission, typically employing SSL (secure sockets layer) encryption. The common *http://* isn't encrypted and is *Not Secure* (as some browsers will explicitly state on the address bar). With HTTPS, a cryptographic key exchange occurs when you first connect to the website. All subsequent actions on the website are encrypted, and thus hidden from prying eyes. Anyone watching can see that you have visited a

---

[28] https://www.howtogeek.com/119723/htg-explains-how-browsers-verify-website-identities-and-protect-against-imposters/

certain website, but cannot see which individual pages you read, or any data transferred.

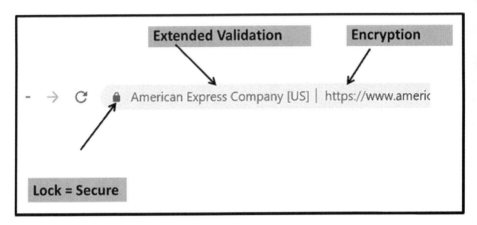

Figure 15 – Website Address Bar Security Clues

I want to go a little more in-depth here just in case you aren't familiar with the structure of a website's address, also known as a *Universal Resource Locator* (URL) – the prototype is http://www.example.com/index.html, where:

- **http** refers to the Hypertext Transfer Protocol, which defines how data to/from the Resource is to be interpreted.
- A **hostname** (www.example.com), also known as a domain name, refers to the name of the Resource. We commonly think of it as a website address. After interpretation, it will typically point to a file directory on the web server (computer) hosting the website's contents, i.e. web pages.
- An optional **file name** (index.html)

Many websites/web pages use http, but they should be avoided, if possible, because they are not encrypted. As previously noted, you should **access https:// web pages whenever possible**, as their use ensures encrypted data traffic both ways.

To increase your https usage (and if you use Chrome™, Firefox™ or Opera® browsers), install the browser add-on *HTTPS Everywhere*, which encrypts communication with many websites – see https://www.eff.org/https-everywhere.

K.1. Minimizing Online Ads

Websites and the companies that provide them track everything you do online. They collect information about your location, browsing habits and more. They utilize the capabilities offered by your browser to implant "cookies" (small files stored on your device) which stores this collected personal information for future use and, most likely, targeted ads. It's called "browser fingerprinting". [29]

Browsers differ in their standard (default) support for this activity. As reported in the Washington Post[30], Google's browser, Chrome, is highly tolerant of "tracker cookies", while Firefox and Safari (on iPhone or Mac), offer much more privacy out-of-the-box.

To minimize this concern (if you are concerned at all), there are a few remedies:

*   Consider switching to a different browser; e.g. Firefox on Windows or Safari on iPhone or Mac.

---

[29] https://en.wikipedia.org/wiki/Device_fingerprint
[30] https://www.washingtonpost.com/technology/2019/06/21/google-chrome-has-become-surveillance-software-its-time-switch/?

- If you don't want to switch browsers, here are two alternate remedies:
  1. Install a browser extension like <u>uBlock Origin</u>, available at https://<u>www.ublockorigin.org</u>. It blocks ads and the data they collect. Combine uBlock with <u>Privacy Badger</u> , available at https://<u>www.eff.org/privacybadger</u>, to reduce tracking ads in addition.
  2. Major browsers, such as Chrome™ and Safari®, offer settings to go *private*. This means that there will be a reduced data trail recorded of where you go on the Internet when these settings are selected.

- Chrome on Windows: clicking on ⋮ and then "*New Incognito Window*" establishes a private browsing tab.
- Safari on the Mac offers privacy settings under *Safari → Preferences* and on the iPhone under *Settings → Safari.*

If ads still get through, when a pop-up ad seems too good to be true, ignore it – it likely is a scam.

K.2. Shoppers Beware

Everyone should consider establishing accounts at major, official websites before a scammer does it for you. This includes Medicare, Social Security, the IRS, the US Postal Service, your smartphone company, your Internet service provider, your banks, your credit card companies and your investments' provider.

When shopping online, access only trusted, known "stores". If unsure or the store is new, go to the Better Business Bureau's website (www.bbb.org) and check its credentials. A good approach is to read a few online reviews before buying – especially the negative ones. *Seals of approval should be IGNORED – they are easily faked by fraudsters.*

Follow the previous guidance on the browser address bar clues. However, even if the clues indicate valid ownership, the identity verification just means that website belongs to the company it claims to belong to. It may not mean that the company itself or its software is trustworthy. When in doubt, skip it.

When web browsing, **never install browser updates (or really any update) that appear as *alerts*** stating you need to do so. Instead, only install them when directly offered by the browser's auto-update feature or when downloading directly from the browser developer's web site (e.g. www.google.com for Chrome).

K.3. Clean Up Stale Digital Haunts and Personal Data

The less personal material about you on the Internet, the lower your personal cyber risk. So, now is a good time to clean up those stale, unused accounts and reduce useless online personal information.

To get started, take an inventory of your online accounts. To jog your memory, start by using your browser's record-keeping:

1. Chrome Browser: click ⬆ in upper right, click *Settings*, click *Passwords*.
2. Or Safari Browser: click *Preferences*, click *Passwords*.

3. And search *yourself* with Google and Bing (i.e. your name, address, telephone, etc.).
4. And check every smartphone app.
5. And take a quick tour through your received email.

Just in case, also check some commonly used websites, such as:

Airlines (American, Delta, United, etc.), Apple, Banks / Credit Unions (Chase, Bank of America, etc.), Craigslist, Dropbox, eBay, Facebook, FedEx, Google, Groupon, Healthcare (Blue Shield, Cigna, ZocDoc, etc.), Hotels (Marriott, Comfort Inns, Hilton, etc.), Internet Service Providers (Spectrum, GoDaddy, etc.), Intuit, Jdate, LinkedIn, Lyft, Match, Meetup, Mint, Mobile Phone (AT&T, Verizon, Sprint, etc.), Netflix, PayPal, Publications (Wall Street Journal, NY Times, etc.), Spotify, Starbucks, Tax Services (TurboTax), Ticketmaster, Twitter, Uber, US Postal Service, UPS, Vimeo, Yahoo.......

Now, delete or cleanse stale digital haunts and data. For example, delete your Google+ account, because it is now defunct.

Here's some "cleansing" guidance:

- Remove unnecessary data.
- Delete if unused or no longer needed.
- Delete unneeded devices.
- Remove password duplicates.
- Remove any unnecessary third party access (e.g. does that site really need access to my Facebook profile?).

ity for Seniors**
K. Web Browsing

Finally, consider using the DeleteMe feature at www.abine.com to delete your personal information from search engines (like Google) – it will clean out *name, address, age, phone number and email address.*

67

L. Social Media

Per Pew Research, 69% of all US adults use at least one social media site[31]. Today's seniors – you readers! - grew up without it. It dominates social interaction for the nation's and much of the world's youth. There is at least one famous senior citizen who uses social media daily to communicate worldwide!

Here's a true cautionary tale: my son, whose business is computer service, recently received a text from what he thought was a Facebook friend. Turns out that the source of the text was an unknown scammer who only *masqueraded* as his Facebook™ friend; that is, he created a Facebook page that borrowed/copied photos, etc. from the real person, then proceeded to attempt a small scam with my son. My son though, canny cyber person that he is, telephoned the real friend just to check and, of course, was informed that there was nothing to this, stopping the scam before it was painful. The impostor Facebook friend used essentially a "spam account" (a fake account).

The foregoing is but one example of such charades. It leads to the conclusion that everything you post on social media has the potential to become public and misused. Further, such is the essence of the Internet: little can be taken back once it's posted. We also know that it's very easy for people to take comments out of context – whether offline or online. So reflect before you post. Consider your online presence from the perspective of family, friends and colleagues (business, volunteerism, etc.).

---

[31] http://www.pewresearch.org/topics/social-media/

Even our involuntary "posts" can be a source of concern today. As reported in the NY Times [32], "most of us are not aware that platforms like Google and Facebook may track and analyze our every search, location, like, video, photo, post and punctuation mark the better to try to sway us." Thus is borne a new, concerning term: "surveillance capitalism."

Social media applications offer privacy controls to determine who can view what content, what can be shared and what not. Spend some time on each application/site to set the privacy settings to what you're comfortable with.

L.1. Facebook™

Use the same privacy practices mentioned above when dealing with Facebook and all the social networks you use. Find this on Facebook under *Settings → Security*. A careful scrub of all Facebook settings should be done periodically.

My wife, friends and I frequently post personal photos for sharing on Facebook. This has been driven by the convenience of smartphone cameras in our pockets and purses. I have especially been taken by the *geo-tagging* of my photos when I review them. Most of us readily forget where we were when we had dinner with Aunt Florence. No more! Geo-tagging is now the default. There is a hidden risk to this seemingly innocent improvement - this information is embedded into the metadata of photos. So, when you share your geo-tagged photos on Facebook, the geo data

---

[32] https://www.nytimes.com/2019/01/18/books/review/shoshana-zuboff-age-of-surveillance-capitalism.html

may help the bad guys locate you or, worse, determine that you are not at home!! The solution is to simply accept the risk or do the following to turn off geo-tagging in your photos:

- iPhone: Settings → Privacy → Location Services → Camera → Never.
- Android: Settings → General → Save Location OFF.

L.2. Linkedin®

For those of us wishing to maintain contact with former work colleagues, LinkedIn serves well. Carefully review your profile to ensure that your persona is accurately represented for both private and public sharing with just the right amount of personal data.

Note – 2FA on LinkedIn is available in the Privacy section.

L.3. Twitter

Again, spend time with the *Settings and Privacy* section. Issues, such as whether tweets should be private or public and whether to reveal your location information, are of particular concern.

L.4. Snapchat™

Snapchat is a multimedia smartphone app. Pictures and messages are usually only available for a short time before they become inaccessible to their recipients. The app features "users'

'Stories' of 24 hours of chronological content, along with 'Discover', letting brands show ad-supported short-form content."[33]

It's hot with the youth these days – I must admit that I have never used it. Pay attention to minimizing your profile information if you choose to use it.

L.5. Jumbo App for Privacy Control

It's free, it's Jumbo and it's a "privacy assistant" [34] app for the iPhone and iPad. It helps you clean up your social presence with Facebook, Twitter, Alexa and Google Search by deleting tweets, search histories and voice recordings It limits the visibility of posts. It disables facial recognition and location tracking, turning off targeted ads, protecting facial recordings and protecting against online tracking.

You can these things yourself, but if you are relatively low-tech and feel overwhelmed, give the Jumbo app a try.

---

[33] Snapchat, www.wikipedia.org
[34] https://www.theverge.com/2019/4/9/18300775/jumbo-privacy-app-twitter-facebook?t

L.6. Internet Dating Senior Style

I became a single senior at the age of 59, about 12 years ago (my wife of 39 years passed away suddenly). I was kind of lost and uncertain as to how I would ever find another spouse again. I am not the kind of person to go to bars or nightclubs (nerd), so I figured that I needed to learn how to dance and find someone at an event at a senior center or church. Luckily, my son suggested that I try Internet dating. After some reflection, I decided to take his advice. I put my profile online at a popular dating site and signed up for 6 months. They sent me a list of 360 potential candidates! I winnowed it down to about a hundred likely prospects based on appearance and proximity, but it was just too many. Little did I realize that the women would approach me! I was a "new fish." Net-net, I had ten dates in as many weeks. My third date has now been my wonderful wife for the past 10 years – she "hooked" me and I was thankfully out of the pool!

As an expert "fisherwoman," she has shared sage advice for anyone putting their social life online to find a special someone:

1. No last name, address or phone number in your profile. Use only your first name or a pseudonym.
2. To communicate, start with private messaging in the dating app you select.
3. Once trust is established, you can graduate to regular texting, email, or actually meeting in person (starting in a public place)!

I would offer a personal profile recommendation: only include a *current* photograph. I was meeting a woman at a restaurant for my 5th date and I was early. In walked a woman I didn't recognize, but suspected that this was my date. Sure enough, it was – her profile photo must have been taken twenty or thirty years earlier. There was no second date.

At the end of the day, it comes down to common sense. Three tipoffs that your "sweetheart" is a likely scam artist:

1. Claims love at first sight.
2. Claims to be from the U.S., but somehow is overseas.
3. Asks for money.

Finally, here is a terrifying cautionary tale: a woman fell for a "romance" scam and became the unknowing "middle-man" in a $500,000 fraud. Her "lover" got the money; she got a 10-year suspended sentence and had to make restitution. [35]

---

[35] https://www.fbi.gov/contact-us/field-offices/losangeles/news/press-releases/business-owner-who-participated-in-business-e-mail-compromise-fraud-scheme-sentenced-to-10-years-in-state-prison

M. Email & Snail Mail

Now we turn to the most used of cyber applications, email.

Reading, sending and receiving email is relatively secure as messages are encrypted during transmission. However, the servers where our emails are stored by our service provider (e.g. Google, Microsoft, Yahoo) are typically unencrypted and may be vulnerable to hackers if our password is compromised – follow the previous recommendations on password creation and changing to minimize this risk.

Our biggest risk with email is being able to recognize email spam. For example, in Figure 16 below, the email looks innocent enough, but upon close inspection, we discern some concerning traces of deception. Note the misspelling of the word Priority in the first line – it's a clear sign that the email sender was sloppy and a key indicator that American Express did NOT originate this note. But if you read it quickly, you might miss this tipoff.

Looking farther down the note, what appears to be a valid website address for American Express is actually a misspelled version – note the extra, inserted "i". In more sophisticated spam versions, the website appears correct, but your personal computer is interpreting/displaying a text protocol called HTML, hiding the real, actionable criminal website address. For example: you see www.americanexpress.com on screen, but behind the scenes (hidden in the HTML) is the hacker's website, www.ransomyourfiles.com. **In most cases, you can "mouse**

over" the link and a pop-up should display the real (behind the scenes) website address. Don't click on this link!!

Subject: **Prirority** Message

From: "American Express"

To: stevek

Date: 11/06/2018 03:08 PM
Dear Member,

You have an urgent important document regarding your American Express card services. Visit our secure server below to read.

http//www.americaniexpress.com/document/read
Thanks.
American Express

Figure 16 - Spam Example from "American Express"

As discussed earlier, a spam email is the first step in a possible ransomware scam. Ransomware attacks are typically carried out using a Trojan virus that is disguised as a legitimate file, contained in an email attachment. Once activated, the ransomware encrypts your personal data and the scammer withholds the decrypting password until a ransom is paid.

Finally, we see in **Figure 17** a very innocent-looking email from Yoka, a personal friend. There's a happy little link after the phrase "Just made my day." Who knows where it will lead? Many friendly messages offer no true personal indicators of legitimacy while many spam messages go to lengths to appear safe. When in doubt, ask your friend for details or just delete. Turning this guidance around, when you want to share a link, a file, a joke, etc. with your family, friends and colleagues, add a personal touch to the email so that *they* are sure it's not spam.

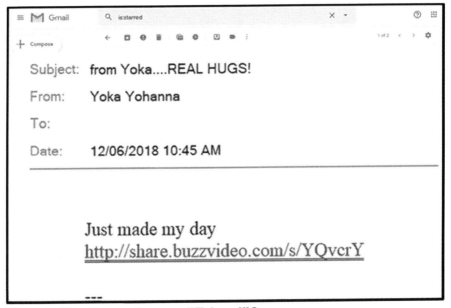

Figure 17 - Spam from a "Friend"?

All of this is designed to lower your guard so you'll be more apt to click a link to a fraudulent website or an attachment. This allows the scammers to download malicious software onto your personal computer or gain access to your passwords and usernames.

A first step to prevent spam "temptation" is to avoid it in the first place. Email programs offer simple methods to *filter* your email, for example:

- In Gmail®, open a concerning email message, click the "3-dot colon" icon on the far right of the email, click on *Block*, *Report Spam* or *Report Phishing* options.

Of course, delete spam emails as soon as they are received. Responding to them just adds to your risk. **Never click on an attachment or a link unless you are 100% sure of its friendly source**. As previously discussed, link addresses may appear benign but may actually hide nefarious addresses. If you are in any way tempted to click on a link, open your browser, *type the link address* yourself or retrieve it from your bookmarks (appending any qualifiers as needed) and go.

M.1. Consider Paying for Your Email Service

Most of us take advantage of **free** email accounts with Google, Microsoft or Yahoo. As we know, you get what you pay for, ladies and gentlemen. If your email is important to you – stores important records, for example – it is wise to upgrade to a business account for a nominal monthly fee (e.g. $6). This typically provides timely support and improved control in a hacking situation. It can mean the difference between preservation of important personal data or total loss.

M.2. Reduce Stored Emails

Despite their sealed envelope imagery, stored email messages are easy for undesired readers (scammers) to exploit – if they get access.

When I led IBM's IT infrastructure in the early 2000's, I added a feature to our worldwide email software that "expired" email messages automatically based on management-approved criteria. The goals were, first, to minimize legal exposure and, second, to minimize wasted space. I was very unpopular for this decision! Unfortunately, I am not aware of a commercial offering with this feature to simplify *email expiration* for the non-business user.

The idea in an email retention policy for casual use should be "do I really need to keep this stuff?" The risk is that nearly any piece of personal data available to an attacker may be used to access other areas of your personal life, leading to identity theft or similar problems. So, an annual purge is a sound idea.

To simply reduce email overhead, consider using the archive features provided by email programs such as Gmail.

My personal practice is to file important emails and attached files in "annual" folders on my laptop, appropriately named. This has proved useful for annual chores such as tax filings (file protection will be discussed later in this presentation). It just makes sense to delete emails with personal information (e.g. SSNs) that aren't of future interest for record-keeping.

M.3. A Few Words About Old-Fashioned Snail Mail

Our neighborhood uses the NextDoor app which supports neighbors sharing requests for local help, recommendations and warnings. This arrived the other day: "I saw this person going through the trash cans in the alley. I saw her going through the black trash cans collecting paperwork and throwing the rest into the blue recycling bins. She had no bags of aluminum cans or 2 liter bottles. When she got to my neighbor's trash, I recorded her and let her know I was watching her so she would know that neighbors look out for neighbors around here. She was not happy to be on camera. *Please shred all your paperwork.*"

Whenever I receive a paper mail (snail mail) credit card offer with my name printed on it, I am careful to shred it. This minimizes the risk of garbage skimmers – like the sweetheart above – applying for it in my name. Ditto for any other commercial offerings that include my name. This should be your standard practice for *any paper records* that you wish to throw out.

There is a new service offered by the US Post Office for snail mail called *Informed Delivery*. It lets you see what's expected to arrive in your mailbox. If there is a check in the mail or an important package, you will be notified. It's a good idea to sign up for the service to pre-empt thieves who might sign up in your stead and swipe your important mail before you see it. For more details, see https://informeddelivery.usps.com . Note that USPS employees will never ask for your username or your password. Do not willingly reveal your credentials to anyone that asks.

Up next is *texting*, which our children and grandchildren have made the new standard for immediate communication. The irony is that it not only the most physically dangerous to use ("Don't drive intoxicated, don't drive intexticated!"[36]), it's also the riskiest from an online communications security perspective.

---

[36] https://www.calif.aaa.com/automotive/distracted-driving.html

N. Texting

For those of us seniors who have spent half a lifetime leaving and listening to voice-mail messages, texting is either a godsend or an irritation. Personally, I prefer texting as a more efficient way to communicate now. It's simple and apparently innocent of problems. If I have a cell phone number of family, friends or colleagues, I can send and receive text messages quickly and easily. Both sender and receiver have the convenient option of reading/not reading the contents immediately or later.

This said, **don't send social security numbers, or other personal information, in text messages**. With the exception of iPhone-to-iPhone communication (which is encrypted), **text messages are NOT encrypted** either in transmission or in storage on the provider's servers. Refer to section V.2. Data Transmission & Storage Security for an overview of each communication alternative and its relative security.

N.1. Have You Been Smished?

We discussed *phishing* previously – an attack using email spam. Of course, scammers' brains never rest – they now send spam text messages, if they know our phone numbers. As with email spam, don't click on links or images from an unknown source of a text.

I have received several *smishes* from scammers seeking to purchase a property that I have never owned. I have been careful about avoiding clicking on an included link, as should you. One click could infect your smartphone and allow criminals to peek at your address book and browsing activity. Be wary!

If you get smished (I smile every time I think this), you can just forward the text message to 7726 to report it and try to block future such junk. 7726 is the *shortcode*[37] (a 5-6 digit number used to send SMS texts) for the GSMA's (Global Speciale Mobile Association) Spam Reporting Service.[38] AT&T, T-Mobile, Verizon, Sprint and Bell™ customers can use this free of charge.

Next we turn to that old standby, the Personal Computer, which many of us have been using for decades. It gets faster with new bells and whistles, like touchscreens, but it's essentially a tool for the suite of applications we have just discussed, like Web browsing and email.

---

[37] A short code is a five-or-six-digit phone number people for texting to subscribe to a texting campaign or to take part in a survey.
[38] https://www.nytimes.com/2018/08/15/smarter-living/how-to-block-spam-calls-texts.html

O. Personal Computers

Most modern personal computer operating systems offer, as standard, a suite of security and privacy functions. The Windows® suite includes most of the standard features, including access control, antivirus, firewall, backup, parental control and storage/disk tune-up. macOS® includes access control, backup (Time Machine), firewall and location control as standard features. Given its superior design, the use of antivirus software on the Mac may be of limited value.

Several commercial offerings compete, from companies such as Norton, McAfee and Bitdefender. Based on PC Magazine's review[39], the commercial competitors are generally superior to "pre-installed" offerings. Some commercial suites include additional functions, such as a password manager and a VPN.

It may seem inconvenient, but relent when your personal computer asks to update your operating system software. Keeping it up to date can be crucial in maintaining the security of your system(s). The risk is that if a vulnerability in a service or application you use is discovered, it can be used to exploit your device and its contents. So, **always keep your software up to date on your smartphone or personal computer**.

---

[39] https://www.pcmag.com/article2/0,2817,2369749,00.asp

O.1. Physical Access Control

Physical access to your personal computer needs attention too. If there is unauthorized access at home or away (e.g. your personal computer is stolen), the thieves can search the data on the hard drive (permanent storage) for personal information. So, follow the previous guidance on passwords (and sometimes pin numbers) on your personal computer's login screen.

In addition, set your personal computer to lock after a short time of inactivity. Close the lid whenever leaving it. If there is realistic, ongoing risk of theft, the *Prey*[40] application should be installed in advance to facilitate recovery.

O.2. Disk (Storage) Encryption

Both major personal computer flavors – Windows or Mac – support **file encryption on fixed and external disks** (e.g. flash drives). It is very important to activate this in case your laptop is stolen. Use BitLocker® (for Windows) or FileVault® (for macOS).

Even more risky is the possible theft or loss of a flash drive – those key-like fobs with a USB connector that plug into any laptop for file sharing. Data should be minimized to the needed files and wiped often. Of course, encrypt as suggested above.

---

[40] https://preyproject.com/

84

O.3. How do I securely dispose of my old personal computer?

First, ask yourself: is my old personal computer useful to anyone? Your grandchildren, perhaps? If not, just destroy the hard drive; e.g. put a few drill holes in it or remove it and smash it with a hammer, done. Then recycle the remains per your local process.

If it is a worthy hand-me-down, transfer all important personal files to your new personal computer. This can be done conveniently by professionals at the store where you are purchasing your new personal computer or by a contracted professional (see V.1. Consulting a Professional). I recommend this approach, if you have never done it before.

Alternatively, if you have experience with migration, you can use the software that comes with your new personal computer – both Windows and macOS offer this. Another option, if you have a complete backup elsewhere, e.g. Carbonite or a Cloud service, is to use it to restore the contents on the new personal computer.

Now, erase ALL contents on your old personal computer's hard disk. It's not as easy as it may sound – you may ask, why not just do a "delete all?" It turns out that you actually need to overwrite the contents of the hard disk completely to ensure that all prior data is obscured. There are several free tools available to do this, such as DBAN (https://dban.org/). This is important to prevent a scammer from stealing any remaining personal information on your old personal computer.

Finally, donate your old personal computer (or bequeath it to your grandchildren!).

Cyber Security for Seniors
O. Personal Computers

We come now to the "new" world of smartphones and tablets, a device category that we have only recently come to know. Built on the latest technologies of touchscreens, wireless communications and long-lasting batteries, they have revolutionized how we talk to each other and what we now keep in our pants pockets and purses!

P. Smartphones and Tablets

P.1. Physical Device Security

I will avoid the clichéd remarks regarding a senior's forgetfulness, but at least once a week I am unsure of the location of my smartphone. If my wife is home, I ask her to call it and hopefully the ring will reverberate through our house! Now that I have sensitized you to this issue, let me offer guidance on maintaining the physical device security of your smartphone.

It is startling to know how easy it is for a smartphone or tablet thief to get past your device's numeric passcode. Per a welivesecurity.com article[41], twenty-six percent of devices could be opened from a set of about 20 candidate numbers!

iPhone (and iPad) users should setup Touch ID® and a non-obvious, non-personal, numeric passcode containing a memorable six digits (or as many as your iPhone allows). Most of the time, Touch ID with your thumb will work just fine. Later iPhones offer Face ID® for improved security. Once you have created a passcode, the iPhone will encrypt your smartphone data, by default. Set the iPhone to erase smartphone contents after 10 failed passcode attempts are made (see *Settings →General → Reset*).

---

[41] https://www.welivesecurity.com/2019/06/19/change-birthday-hackers-may-know-pin/

Android users should set up fingerprint recognition to unlock the smartphone by going to *Settings → Lock screen and security → Fingerprint scanner.* In addition, setup a non-obvious PIN code or alphanumeric passcode by going to *Settings → Security → Screen lock.* Finally, encrypt the contents on your smartphone by going to *Settings → Security & Location → Encryption → Encrypt phone → enter lock screen PIN or password.*

Take advantage of the **Lock Screen on your smartphone to provide an email address and an alternate smartphone number** in case your lost or stolen smartphone is recovered by a good Samaritan. Simply use a graphic editor on your lock screen photo to add the needed information (Windows offers Paint free, out-of-the-box). In **Figure 18**, you see a current photo of my beautiful wife for my smartphone's lock screen. It includes a telephone number and an email address at the bottom for a possible good Samaritan to connect with and return my lost smartphone.

818 -123-1234
myemail@gm.com

Figure 18 - Lock Screen for Good Samaritan

In the event that your smartphone is stolen, there is a possible recovery solution if the thief doesn't turn the smartphone off (and then reset it):

- For iPhones, it's the *Find My iPhone* app;
- For Androids, it's the *Find My Device* feature.

P.2. Location Sharing

There is reason for concern about the use of your personal location data generated by your smartphone. For example, your location data can leak your home or work address to the wrong people. Similarly, if you are at a public location, it can signal that your home is unoccupied to thieves.

Publicly sharing your location can signal someone to meet you in a public venue unintentionally. It's a "hot commodity" as reported in the NY Times in December, 2018[42]. Per the AARP Bulletin, location data can also come from listening to music (smart speakers), watching TV (smart TVs), and cooking a meal (smart appliances)!!! [43]

Several technologies are being used by smartphone apps[44], to track your location for marketing purposes. The most precise is Bluetooth, which can locate you inside a store and direct you to the latest product sale,

---

[42] https://www.nytimes.com/interactive/2018/12/10/business/location-data-privacy-apps.html
[43] https://www.aarp.org/money/scams-fraud/info-2018/where-companies-are-tracking-data.html
[44] https://www.nytimes.com/interactive/2019/06/14/opinion/bluetooth-wireless-tracking-privacy.html?action=click&module=Opinion&pgtype=Homepage

Note, that even without authorizing sharing, smartphone (cell phones) can be tracked through cell towers and/or Wi-Fi networks.

If you prefer not to turn off location services entirely, make an active choice as to what situations are warranted. Limit use to apps that must know it; e.g. WAZE®, a GPS navigation app.

P.3. Contact Sharing

Access to your Contacts should be minimized as well. In the wrong hands, your contacts can reveal personal information of friends, relatives and colleagues to the wrong persons. Another risk: if the social media site that stores your contacts gets hacked, your contact list may become public.

On the iPhone, go to *Settings → Privacy → Contacts* to see which apps can access your contacts. Adjust as needed.

On the Android, the native Contacts app by Google provides a consistent interface between your smartphone and the web, and it links closely with social media apps like Facebook. Individual contacts can be selectively unshared.

P.4. Telephone Account Access

You may have had a cell phone for decades with AT&T or Verizon and never knew that you could get a pin to control access to the account. Getting one prevents a scammer from setting up a separate account in your name, essentially masquerading as you. Once a pin is set up with your carrier, for example Verizon®, they will demand it for any future account interactions.

P.5. Vishing (Spam Calls)

I get at least 4 calls per day from random telephone numbers, most of them are sales persons, some of them scams. I have just learned a new name for this experience – *vishing*, the v for voice version of phishing.

A troubling vishing trend is called "spoofing," where web-based calling technology is used to make the caller's number appear to be local – the reasoning is that it will make the receiver more likely to answer. In some cases, these "local" numbers are real numbers, borrowed from a local business or person by the scammer. [45]

If this is personal issue for you, telephone vendors offer various services at relatively modest prices to minimize these calls. I ignore these calls and assume that, if they are legitimate, they will leave a voice mail message. In parallel, I make it a practice to add all known persons to my *Contacts* as soon as possible – this minimizes ignored calls that should have been answered.

---

[45] Wall Street Journal, Jan 2, 2019

A familiar scam call comes from a so-called technical expert targeting Windows users and requesting access to your personal computer to solve a problem. For the truly gullible, the scammer will seek and gain credit card and financial information resulting in painful losses.

P.6. Guidance to Minimize Vishing (Spam Calls)

There are assorted approaches to minimize vishing attacks, starting with your telephone service provider:

- Verizon offers a "Caller Name ID" app to identify spam/robo calls as they arrive ($3/mo).
- T-Mobile®, AT&T® and Sprint™ offer call blocking.
- The Google Pixel™ smartphone can be set to block known spam numbers.

For additional ways to minimize vishing, check out these resources:

- The Cellular Telecommunications Industry (CTIA) provides guidance on stopping robocalls at www.ctia.org/consumer-resources/how-stop-robocalls.
- The Federal Trade Commission (FTC) offers tips at www.fcc.gov/consumers/guides and
- Use the "Do Not Call" Registry by calling 888-382-1222 or going to https://www.donotcall.gov/.

P.7. Migrate from Old to New Smartphone (Securely)

The simplest and safest approach is to ask your service provider to do an in-store setup and migration from your old to your new smartphone. If somehow you have acquired a new smartphone outside of a retail purchase, consider seeking a professional (see V.1. Consulting a Professional) to help you perform the setup and migration to avoid painful data loss.

In the meantime, for you gutsy seniors with iPhones out there, try this to backup all data (if not previously doing such):

1. Open Settings on your old iPhone.
2. Click the top menu item - it should be your name.
3. Click *iCloud* and turn on any APPS USING ICLOUD that you want on your new smartphone.
4. Click *iCloud Backup → Back Up Now.* Turn your old iPhone off once the backup is finished.

For you gutsy seniors with Android smartphones out there, try this to backup all data (if not done already):

1. Tap on *Settings → Tap Backup & reset → Enter your PIN → Swipe on "Backup my data" and "Automatic restore" → Tap Backup Account → Tap Google Account Name → Return to Settings menu.*
2. Tap Accounts → Tap Google → Select your Gmail account → Swipe on preferences for items to backup (including App Data, Calendar, Chrome, Contacts, Docs, Drive) → Return to Settings menu.

3. To backup Photos and Videos: Tap Photos app → Tap 3 horizontal line icon in upper left → Sign into Gmail account → Return to Settings menu → Return to Photos app main screen → Tap Settings → Tap Backup & sync → Switch on Backup option → Tap Backup all.

Remove any SD or SIM cards from your old smartphone if you're going to move them to your new one. If you aren't going to move them, delete all contents.

Make sure that you can re-access the backup/cloud data on your new smartphone. This should get you up and running.

Erase all remaining contents on your old smartphone by doing a factory reset as follows:

- For the iPhone, go to *Settings → General → Reset* .
- For the Android, *Tap Settings → Backup & reset → Tap Factory data reset and Reset phone →* Enter pass code → Erase everything.
- Before you let your old smartphone go, double check that all personal information is gone.

Finally, now that it's effectively dead, consider recycling or donating your old smartphone. Your carrier, e.g. AT&T or Verizon, may offer this option. Sadly, your grandchildren likely won't want it....

The next chapter focuses on the very personal, and crucial, area of our identity: our credit and keeping track of our finances. It may be the most important part of the book.

Q. Financial

Q.1. Protect Your Identity

Identity theft, per Wikipedia, is "the theft of personally identifying information, generally including a person's name, date of birth, social security number, driver's license number, bank account or credit card numbers... or any other information that can be used to access a person's financial resources." If the thief is successful, our worst fears are realized and we may have a multiple months-long journey to reverse the results.

With the recent Equifax breach, it becomes imperative to take steps to protect your identity, especially when it touches your financial resources.

Here is my suggested guidance:

- **Do Frequent Monitoring** - I have been using the Quicken® application on my Windows laptop to do a daily check of my transactions and account balances for many years. On one fortuitous occasion, I saw a $500 withdrawal from my checking account that I hadn't made. Turned out, I used my debit card one day to buy gas and it was "skimmed" from the pump by a thief at a local Arco station. By realizing this within a day, I was able to cancel the card and the bank refunded the loss that week. As a result, I stopped using that gas station and resolved to continue to use Quicken daily to monitor all my accounts. Quicken operates on multiple platforms (Windows,

Mac, Web, etc.) and offers a convenient, secure and quick solution for account monitoring and transactions.

- Another alternative is using one of your financial institution's websites to organize and collect all of your accounts. My personal investment company's website allows account consolidation for checking, savings, investments and credit cards as well – from an assortment of providers.

- **Dedicate a single device** to all financial activities to minimize risk. I use my laptop for everything financial at home.

- **Set up account alerts** for each of your credit and debit cards. For example, American Express offers a slew of alerts, either email or text. They include alerts for irregular activity, foreign transactions, card not present, large purchase and cash withdrawal. I particularly appreciate the text alerts as they are immediate and, depending on your setup, happily intrusive.

- **Freeze Your Credit File** - If your personal information is stolen, thieves can use your personal information to make loans or set up new credit cards in your name at their address. You won't receive bills, so your first clue that something is a problem will likely be a collection agency hounding for unpaid bills or delinquent charges that you didn't make. You will likely think these are the previously described scam cold calls, but sadly they will not be!

- So, *freeze your credit file* at the websites of Equifax (www.equifax.com) , Experian (www.experian.com), TransUnion (www.transuniuon.com) and Innovis™ (www.innovis.com). ***Each will give you a PIN Number – store it in a safe place for unfreezing/refreezing***. This should prevent a thief from making a loan or opening a credit card without your knowledge. All credit freezes are free thanks to a new federal law. You can selectively unfreeze for new credit needs from _new_ creditors; then refreeze when their needs are satisfied. A freeze doesn't impact prior and current creditors.

- If needed, freeze at the National Consumer Telecommunications and Utilities Exchange which is used by telecommunication companies to determine customer credit (http://www.nctue.com/). It too offers a freeze via a telephone call to 866-349-5355.

- You are entitled to **receive a free copy of your credit report** once every 12 months through AnnualCreditReport.com from each of the 4 major credit bureaus – Equifax™, Transunion®, Experian™ and Innovis™. Take advantage of this to determine your status _every four months_ during the year.

- **File your taxes early** - A scary example of identity theft is a scammer filing "your" taxes for you! Unfortunately, _they_ collect the "refund." So, file your taxes as early as possible. Get organized early and submit your return as soon as you receive your statements: 1098s, 1099s, W2s, Social Security, interest, dividends, etc.

Q.2. Do I Need Identity Theft Insurance?

The cyber security industry has responded to the identity theft threat with products such as _identity theft insurance_. For a monthly fee ($10-20), they will monitor and perhaps remedy such theft. You may be bombarded by ads for these products at the same time front-page news headlines trumpet new personal data breaches. So, should you buy an insurance policy against identity theft?

Somewhat happily, the actual incidents of identity theft are relatively low – per Wikipedia, up to 2% of the results of a data breach[46]. Per Consumer Reports®[47], less than 1% of the victims suffer any serious loss.

Victims of identity theft spent roughly seven hours resolving problems associated with the crime[48]. Since banks and credit-card companies typically reimburse people for unauthorized account use, only 14% of victims actually lost money with a typical loss of only $100.

Our recommended guidance to *freeze your credit files will mitigate most of the need for identity theft insurance.* Consumer Reports® considers identity theft insurance a waste of money.

Q.3. Making Payments Securely in the 21st Century

I am writing fewer and fewer checks every year. In 2018, I wrote less than 15 physical checks. Most of my transactions were online and credit card-based, with a few monthly payments drawn directly from my checking account.

---

[46] Identity Theft, www.wikipedia.org
[47]
https://www.consumerreports.org/video/view/money/news/2245992247001/skip-identity-theft-protection-services/
[48] https://www.bjs.gov/content/pub/pdf/vit14_sum.pdf

Online transactions through a web browser allow many of us to perform our financial obligations securely and efficiently. We previously discussed the importance of passwords and 2FA to add the needed access security. As previously discussed, try to make financial transactions only with https websites; that is, websites with secure, encrypted data transfer enabled by the https protocol.

When I am in a store, I rarely use cash, rarely use a debit card and never use paper checks – I use one of my credit cards. With new technology comes an improvement – "mobile" payments using a smartphone. Called variously Apple Pay®[49], Samsung Pay®[50] or Google Pay®[51], mobile payments using *Near Field Communication* (or NFC) are more secure than traditional credit card transactions, even the new digital-chip-in-card kind.

With a debit card or a credit card connected to the digital wallet app in your smartphone, NFC allows information to pass between your device and a retailer's payment terminal when they are "near" one another (a few inches). Most *major* retailers support this at checkout. Given that this is an emerging technology, you will have to ask the cashier if it's available.

Most Android®, Apple®, and Samsung® smartphones have a digital wallet. Apple Pay®, Google Pay™ and Samsung Pay® apps use this.

---

[49] https://support.apple.com/en-us/HT204003
[50] https://www.samsung.com/us/support/owners/app/samsung-pay
[51] https://support.google.com/pay/answer/7644134?hl=en

Each transaction uses a unique, random transaction number—instead of your account or credit card number. Your account information is encrypted, and can only be accessed via password or, with some smartphones, your fingerprint. A neat advantage is that if your card or its information is ever lost or stolen, banks can issue a new one to your smartphone immediately – no waiting for the mail. If your smartphone is lost or stolen, follow previous guidance on securing and, possibly, recovering it.

With fingerprint recognition on your smartphone, you hold your smartphone near the payment terminal while your fingertip is on the power button. A vibration and beep will confirm your payment and a transaction record magically appears in your digital wallet.

I have just started using my Apple Pay Wallet app and I love it. Instead of pulling out my wallet and credit card at checkout, I pull out my iPhone, unlock it with Touch ID (my thumbprint), open my Wallet app, click on the desired card, and, with my thumb on the fingerprint reader button, hold my iPhone near the payment terminal – the cashier hands me a receipt. *Sometimes you will have to train the checkout person to get started - a fun role reversal for a grey-haired senior vs. hip millennial!* ☺

Stuff – most of us have lots of it, especially the really senior among us. The next chapter, Files and Records, hones in on what to keep, what to discard and how best to do it.

R. Files and Records

Based on my decades-long, annual interaction with the IRS, I know to keep my tax records and other important financial documents for at least 3 years. A more personal choice is keeping photos, videos and music for a lifetime, unless they prove to be embarrassing or too voluminous.

R.1. What to Keep and How Long to Keep It?

- Email – consider an annual purge to minimize the risk of unnecessary personal data being exposed, in case of a hacker breach.
- Browser History & Cookies – your browser history is what your web browser of choice records to improve future response time. Cookies are small files on your personal computer (or smartphone) that a website uses to keep track of your personal information when you return. It makes sense to clear these files at least annually to minimize risk of nefarious use of the history and cookies by hackers.

    - In Chrome: *History → History → Clear Browsing Data*

    - In Safari Mobile: *Settings → Safari → Clear History and Website Data*

- Tax, business, financial and legal records – Per the IRS, you should keep tax records for 3 years in most cases[52]. Given that these are increasingly originated and/or stored online,

---

[52] https://www.irs.gov/businesses/small-businesses-self-employed/how-long-should-i-keep-records

101

keeping all of these indefinitely is an easy option. I maintain annual directories on my laptop's hard drive to organize these important files. I also use the scanner in my multi-function printer to convert paper-originated documents to images for record-keeping purposes.

- Photos, Videos, Music – personal preference, but generally forever as long as there is space!

R.2. Backup/Recovery

Backup and recovery of files mitigates device theft, device loss, device failure, ransomware attacks and data overflow. There are important alternatives to consider:

- *No backup* (or the ostrich approach) is the easiest, but is highly risky! Consider that a dead smartphone or a stolen personal computer means total loss....

- *Local backup* is conveniently handled by a USB-connected inexpensive external storage device coupled with the following software alternatives to perform the data backup:

  - Mac offers "Time Machine"

  - Windows 10 offers "Backup using File History"

  However, consider the many disasters that may occur that could destroy not only the primary file storage but also destroy a local backup. This implies that a **remote backup strategy is a better approach**.

- **Remote backup** – this means using the Internet to (continuously) transfer files from your personal computer to a remote server. Choosing this alternative is, ultimately, the best solution if disasters, like floods, hurricanes and earthquakes, are possible in your area (like pretty much everywhere!).

  - A common choice is to use Cloud services. See the table, Cloud and Backup/Recovery Services, below for a list of commercial alternatives. An advantage of cloud service usage is the ability to share files across one or more devices.

  - My personal choice for several years has been Carbonite™. It runs on my Windows laptop in the background and sends me a monthly email report of its activities.

R.3. Storage Overflow

A common consideration is how to handle storage overflow on one's device (or "Help, I ran out of space!"). As storage has become cheaper, decade by decade, most of us rarely encounter overflow. Nevertheless, it should be considered before the issue arises.

Users can periodically delete extraneous files to avoid overflow or just use the "cloud" as suggested in the table below. An advantage of cloud service usage is the ability to share files across one or more devices.

Cloud and Backup/Recovery Services

App	Company	Cost	Pros	Cons	Devices
iCloud	Apple	5GB free, $2/mo- 50GB, 2TB for $10/month	Best for Apple, syncs calendar, contacts, etc.	Hard to use for non-Apple	All
OneDrive ™	Microsoft	5GB free, 1TB for $7/month	Best for PCs		All
Google-Drive	Google	15GB free, 2TB for $10/month	Best for online Google users		All
Dropbox™	Dropbox	2GB free, 1TB for $10/month	Best for large files	Data security concerns[53]	All
Norton 360	Symantec	25GB included; additional 50GB= $60/yr	Part of good "suite"; shareable	Expensive vs. standalone	All
Carbonite	Carbonite	$6/month	Unlimited storage	Just Backup/ recovery	PCs, Macs

---

[53] https://www.legaltechnology.com/latest-news/security-comment-why-are-people-still-using-dropbox-for-business/

S. Kicking the Bucket

As a senior, I am especially sensitive to end of life considerations. I worry daily about my loved ones and what the impact of my death will have on them. Perhaps **the most important of my contributions in this book is to highlight a responsible, effective and secure approach to enable a successful transition of an *online life* to my heirs.**

The traditional transition documents are Wills, Trusts, Durable Power of Attorney, Advanced Health Care Directive, Life Insurance policies and Burial/Funeral Instructions. I am not an attorney, so I can offer no guidance on these. This said, I created my will, my advanced health care directive, my wife's will and her living trust with *WillPower* software a few years ago. If you have a simple financial situation, this may serve you well.

I suggest a **cyber in the event of my death letter** be written to facilitate the transition of an online life to one's heirs, with the following contents:

- Personal Computer(s) and Smartphone(s) Access instructions, such as passwords and pins.

- Critical File/Record access

    - Backup files, disks and Cloud accounts.

    - Tax documents, such as TurboTax® files.

- Online Accounts IDs/Passwords including password manager ID and password, if any.

- Contacts and access details to the following:

    - Life Insurance policies

    - Investments

    - Banks – Checking and Savings Accounts

    - Mortgages, Loans

    - Medicare

    - Pensions

    - Social Security

    - Ongoing Bills – any automatic payments?

Consider combining in a package with:

- Copies of traditional key documents

- Safe Deposit Box Key(s) & Access

Note: A novel feature is available in the LastPass Password Manager to pre-authorize specific people (heirs, executors) to access online accounts, etc.

T. Final Thoughts

It's a dangerous cyber-world out there, be safe!!

Cybercrime is a reality for many individuals, unfortunately. However, most of us will avoid it by following the advice in this book. It includes many common sense practices and technology solutions to help keep you safe.

Refer to the B. Security Checklist for a handy view of do's and don'ts to aid you in your cyber safety journey. As mentioned earlier, a downloadable and printable version is available from my website, **www.nerdsiview.com**.

Finally, challenge yourself with the V.5. Quiz in the Appendix section to see if this book's guidance was helpful. My shot at the answers follow. ☺

I hope the time you spent with this book was worthwhile.

Thanks, Steve.

U. Bibliography

Claypoole and Payton, Protecting Your Internet Identity, Rowman & Littlefield, 2017.

Foreign Policy Association, Toward the Year 2018, Cowles Education Corp., 1968.

Refer to the many footnotes throughout the book for additional references.

V. Appendices

V.1. Consulting a Professional

Most of the security measures listed in the Security Checklist on page 9 can be readily performed by the typical computer user. However, a few *may* require the services of a computer professional, depending on the user's (your) experience:

1. Network and router setup
2. Computer migration
3. Device infection removal (e.g. virus, ransomware)
4. File encryption

In general, the professional will need hands-on to properly diagnose/repair and/or complete the necessary operations. Some cases of device infection and file encryption setup may be handled remotely – over the Internet with the pro taking over device control.

Once you have made the decision to contact a pro, seek referrals from family, friends and colleagues. If several people had a solid experience with one particular service, the chance of you receiving similar service is likely very good.

Short of a trusted referral, an online search is the next step. Many pros have reviews on various services that should make your decision making easier; e.g. Yelp is a great example of a helpful service for this, as is the local business information on Google Maps.

Cyber Security for Seniors
V. Appendices

After you have done your "due diligence" in selecting a skilled pro, here are some important questions to ask and the expected responses:

- How much do you charge per hour? Expect: "We charge _($50-100)__ per hour." Experience of the professional and problem difficulty may impact this.
- How many hours should this take? Expect: "We can't be sure, but this typically takes ___ hours."
- Is there a minimum charge? Expect: "Yes, one hour's rate."
- Are there any charges other than the hourly rate? Expect: "No, in general. New or additional software or hardware will be extra." Consider requesting an estimate.
- Do you charge extra for in-home service? Expect: "Yes, we charge an additional ____ for in-home service."
- Do you guarantee your service? Expect: "Yes, for __(30-90)__ days."
- Will you preserve my files? Expect: "Yes, if they're there, we will save them."
- When will my device be ready? Expect: "24 to 48 hours."

V.2. Data Transmission & Storage Security

What is the relative security of our major online activities – as data flows over the various networks to and from each activity? Following are my general conclusions. For the nerdish readers, refer to the table below in addition.

- **Email** is relatively secure. However, the servers where our emails are stored by our service provider (e.g. Google, Microsoft, Yahoo) are typically unencrypted and may be vulnerable to hackers.
- **Web Browsing** will be relatively secure if you stick with websites that offer the HTTPS protocol (encrypting transmission to and from). However, if the website doesn't protect your data on its servers, you may be vulnerable to hackers.
- **File Transfers** (uploads/downloads) are occasional activities and will be insecure if the FTP protocol is used. In almost all cases, we aren't aware if a secure protocol, such as SFTP, is used.
- **Texts** are unencrypted and insecure. Do not send personal information via text!!
- **Voice** calls are secure in transmission. However, when stored as mailbox messages, the simple 4-digit pin code to gain access can be readily hacked.

Cyber Security for Seniors
V. Appendices

Appli-cation	Network	Trans-mission Protocols	Trans-mission Secure?	VPN Trans-mission Secure?	Server Storage Secure?
Email	Internet*	SMTP, POP, IMAP	Yes, Encrypted	Yes, Encrypted	No, at vendor servers
Web Browsing	Internet*	HTTP, HTTPS	http:/ = No.. https:/ = Yes, encrypted.	Yes	Varies by website.
File Transfer	Internet*	FTP, SFTP	No, not encrypted. Yes, encrypted.	Yes	Varies by website.
Texting	Cellular**	SMS, MMS	No, except iPhone-to-iPhone is Encrypted and secure.	N/A	No, at vendor servers
Voice (cellular)	Cellular**	CDMA, TDMA, ….	Yes, encrypted.	N/A	No, mailbox access by pin #

*__Internet__ means different things depending on the device you are using and where you are using it. If you are using a personal computer or smartphone at home, it means that your device will typically connect to your Wi-Fi network, which, in turn, connects to your ISP's digital Internet connection. If you are using your smartphone outside your home, you are most likely using the cellular data network of your phone provider to connect to the Internet.

**Cellular means the cellular data network of your phone provider to deliver the text or voice capability to your device (e.g. smartphone).

V.3. Fake News

I debated internally about including fake news in this book and discussed it with my son Paul, an attorney. He argued that it didn't pertain to cyber security and should be omitted. As I agreed with his perspective, I decided to compromise – don't include it in the mainline text, but include some explanation and guidance as an appendix.

Fake news is harmful to our online experience. The harm that it causes is internal – in our minds. It starts as personal confusion, eventual acceptance and ultimate transmission to many others. This exponential proliferation has a negative impact on our entire society.

Two personal brushes with fake news from friends:

• "Hillary linked to the murder of 125 people" was relayed to me after my weekly poker game by one of the players, a personal friend who I respected (he is a medical professional). I was stunned and asked how he had learned this – I would assume that if Hillary Clinton was linked to even ONE murder, she would be under arrest and on trial. He told me to "check it out online." I did and discovered this nonsense on some non-descript website. Pure fiction; i.e. fake news.

- Another personal friend recently sent me an email with, among other statements, included: "Alex Jones: getting vaccinated ...increases the risk of diseases spreading." When I responded immediately that Jones was a known purveyor of false information and that this was a very harmful message to send, she responded that she was adamant about these "facts."

My protective guidance is to recognize and challenge fake news in your experience as it occurs – whether in person or online. Here is a guide to recognizing fake news from the International Federation of Library Associations and Institutions[54]:

1. Consider the source (to understand its mission and purpose)

2. Read beyond the headline (to understand the whole story)

3. Check the authors (to see if they are real and credible)

4. Assess the supporting sources (to ensure they support the claims)

5. Check the publication date (to see if the story is relevant and up to date)

6. Ask if it is a joke (to determine if it is meant to be satire)

7. Review your own biases (to see if they are affecting your judgement)

8. Ask experts (to get confirmation from independent people with knowledge).

---

[54] https://www.ifla.org/publications/node/11174

Happily, at least two major cyber media providers are stepping up:

- Facebook now asks independent fact-checking organizations to identify false and misleading information. When users try to post fake news, they see a pop-up that explains the problem and asks confirmation to continue. [55]
- Google is now "adjusting systems to display more trustworthy content." Google has launched the Google News Initiative (GNI) to fight the spread of fake news. "The company is … working to adjust its systems to display more trustworthy content during times of breaking news." [56]

---

[55] https://www.nytimes.com/2018/10/15/opinion/facebook-fake-news-philosophy.html
[56] Fake News, www.wikipedia.org

V.4. Improving Your Home & Travel Security

V.4.1. The Power of a Smart Doorbell

My son lives in a townhouse in the San Fernando Valley. Over two years ago he installed a Ring Video Doorbell [57] outside his front door. It allows him to see callers on his smartphone and record the encounter. So far, no incidents.

Now, I am considering buying one because one of my poker buddies just shared the story of a serious burglary attempt at his home. He was out of the house. His Ring notified him of "visitors" so he starting watching them via live video on his smartphone. When he realized it was a burglary attempt, he sent an alert to his security system to turn on the sirens – this spooked the crooks and they fled. He then telephoned the police. Whew!

If you have concerns about home invasion or just bothersome visitors, the Ring Video Doorbell might be a good investment. It is relatively inexpensive at $199 (on Amazon) and easy to install. PC Magazine gives it a top rating [58].

---

[57] https://support.ring.com/hc/en-us
[58] https://www.pcmag.com/review/359169/ring-video-doorbell-2

V.4.2. OOMA "Landline" with a Security Bonus

I first learned about the OOMA® box when I read an article from Consumer Reports[59] several years ago. They recommended it highly and I invested. *The Ooma Telo (see www.ooma.com) replaced my landline phone for less than $5 per month*! I plugged my home phone system into the Ooma Telo. I plugged the Ooma Telo into my home router and, bingo, with a few simple setup activities my old phone line rang again. Quality is excellent! I have never looked back, despite our near total conversion to cell phone use.

Building on their product success, the Ooma company more recently introduced a very reasonably priced add-on security service to the Ooma Telo. I purchased 3 sensors – a front door sensor, a motion sensor and a water leak sensor. I installed them in a few minutes and, with their Home Security app on my iPhone, can now check if I have a flood or a break-in, etc. The cost is less than $16/month!

---

[59]

https://www.consumerreports.org/video/view/electronics/smartphones/3386137
370001/ooma--super-cheap-phone-service/

V.4.3. Security Tips When Traveling

The digitization of personal data and the Internet intrude everywhere, including in ways to make ourselves *more* secure as we travel. Following is a simple way to accomplish this.

- Scan your itinerary details, driver's license, passport, credit cards (both sides), medical records, medication list and doctors contact information.
- Make sure that your file backup software saves these scanned documents to the Internet where they can be retrieved from anywhere. I can do this with Carbonite.
- Share access with someone at home.
- Print two copies: one for your suitcase (in a plastic bag), the other to someone at home. [60]

---

[60] https://www.fidelity.com/viewpoints/financial-basics/traveling-and-document-security?ccsource=email_weekly

V.5. Quiz

1. Which is the most secure password? Stevekrantz, Schmootz11$, or "My dog Spot has fleas on his belly."

2. Public Wi-Fi (even if password protected) is not always safe for sensitive activities – True or False?

3. What is a phishing attack?

4. Turning off a smartphone GPS function does not prevent all location tracking – True or False?

5. Americans can legally obtain one free credit report yearly from each of the four credit bureaus – True or False?

6. Ransomware involves criminals encrypting and holding users' data hostage until paid – True or False?

7. Wi-Fi traffic is not encrypted by default on all wireless routers – True or False?

8. https:// in a URL means that information entered into the site is encrypted – True or False?

9. A VPN minimizes the risk of using insecure Wi-Fi networks – True or False?

10. What is two factor authentication (2FA) ?

V.6. Quiz Answers

1. Which is the most secure password? Stevekrantz, Schmootz11$, or "My dog Spot has fleas on his belly." The least secure is my name, Stevekrantz, for obvious reasons. The next two are controversial. Schmootz11$ contains a nonsense word, a number and a special character as typically recommended. However, it is very hard to remember. "My dog…" is much longer than either of the others, therefore hard for a scammer to crack. It's the winner, in my opinion, because is it much more MEMORABLE than Schmootz11$.

2. Public Wi-Fi (even if password protected) is not always safe for sensitive activities – True or False? TRUE, because it isn't encrypted. If you must use public Wi-Fi, limit use to non-critical, non-financial activities where no IDs or passwords are transmitted. If you are regularly tempted, invest in a VPN service as discussed earlier in the text.

3. What is a phishing attack? An email with a link to a scammer's website or an attachment containing a virus. A worst case is that a phishing attack can lead to ransomware (see question 6).

4. Turning off a smartphone GPS function does not prevent all location tracking – True or False? TRUE, because smartphone communications can be traced to local cell towers!

5. Americans can legally obtain one free credit report yearly from each of the four credit bureaus – True or False? TRUE. Get one every four months, rotating among the 3 major providers, Experian, Equifax and Transunion.

6. Ransomware involves criminals encrypting and holding users' data hostage until paid – True or False? TRUE. Ransomware involves a virus that you inadvertently download, usually from a phishing attack. Once installed on your personal computer, the virus encrypts your data files so that they are inaccessible until a decryption password is provided by the scammer.

7. Wi-Fi traffic is not encrypted by default on all wireless routers – True or False? TRUE, so it's important when your router is set up, you select WPA2 encryption.

8. https:// in a URL means that information entered into the site is encrypted – True or False? TRUE. You should try to only browse to websites that use https because it is encrypted. See earlier guidance on how to maximize its use on page 61K. Web Browsing.

9. A VPN minimizes the risk of using insecure Wi-Fi networks – True or False? TRUE, a VPN is a Virtual Private Network, channeling your Internet transmissions in encrypted form to and from a private server, thereby minimizing your exposure to hackers.

10. What is two factor authentication (2FA)? In addition to authentication through an ID and password combination, a separate numeric code is sent to a secondary device (e.g. your smartphone) and returned to provide improved security.

W. Glossary

Term	Definition
2FA	See Two-Factor Authentication
AirBnb	Airbnb is an online marketplace which lets people rent out their properties or spare rooms to guests.
AirDrop	An iPhone-to-iPhone feature that uses Bluetooth local communications to share information.
Antivirus Software	Software that will periodically check your personal computer/smartphone memory for dangerous, foreign code or files (small bits of software) and remove or nullify its ability to affect your computer/phone's operation.
App	Short-hand name for a personal computer/smartphone application
App Store	Apple's source for new/additional apps for your iPhone
Back door	A means of regaining access to a compromised system by installing software or configuring existing software to enable remote access under attacker-defined conditions.
Backup/Recovery	Copying selected personal computer files to separate, safe storage with the ability to recover it at a later date/time.
Bluetooth	A personal-area network or PAN for electronic devices to communicate in close proximity.

Cyber Security for Seniors
W. Glossary

Term	Definition
Botnet	A term derived from "robot network"; is a large automated and distributed network of previously compromised computers that can be simultaneously controlled to launch large-scale attacks such as a denial-of-service attack on selected victims.
Browser	An application that supports Internet access of website files, e.g. Safari, Chrome.
Browser fingerprinting	A browser fingerprint is information collected about a remote computing device for the purpose of identification. Fingerprints can be used to fully or partially identify individual users or devices even when cookies are turned off.
Byte	A small amount (8 bits) of digital data, typically representing a single alphabetic or numeric character.
CDMA	Code-Division Multiple Access; a protocol used in 2G and 3G mobile phone communications.
Cellular network	A communication network where the last link is wireless, distributed over land areas called "cells".
Clickjacking	An apparent legitimate link in a social media application or webpage that has been hijacked by a scammer to execute harmful code.

Term	Definition
Cloud computing	Convenient, on-demand network access to a shared pool of resources that can be rapidly provisioned and released with minimal management effort or service provider interaction.
Cookie	A file on your personal computer/smartphone created by a website to store personal information about your use
Cybercrime Support Network	See www.fraudsupport.org for victims of **cybercrime.**
Cybersecurity	The protection of information assets by addressing threats to information processed, stored and transported by internetworked information systems.
Denial of service attack	An assault on a service from a single source that floods it with so many requests that it becomes overwhelmed and is either stopped completely or operates at a significantly reduced rate.
Domain	A unique name typically of the form xxx.yyy which defines an area of control in the internet, e.g. google.com, apple.com, irs.gov
Encryption	The process of taking an unencrypted message (plaintext), applying a mathematical function to it (encryption algorithm with a key) and producing an encrypted message (cypher text)
Extended Verification Certificate (EV)	Issued by Certification authorities indicating extensive verification of the website's identity has taken place. Will see owner name at left in browsers' address bar.

Term	Definition
Firewall	Software and/or hardware that protect a personal computer (or smartphone) from unauthorized data traffic from/to the internet.
Firmware	Software programmed into non-volatile-memory of a device. It typically provides the low-level control for the device's specific hardware
FTP	File Transfer Protocol is used to transfer computer files between a client and server on the Internet.
Google Play™	Google's source for new/additional apps for an Android smartphone
Hacking	The act of attempting to gain unauthorized access/control of another's personal computer/smartphone.
Hypertext Transfer Protocol Secure (HTTPS)	A protocol for accessing a secure web server, whereby all data transferred are encrypted
Hypertext Transfer Protocol (HTTP)	A communication protocol used to connect to servers on the World Wide Web. Its primary function is to establish a connection with a web server and transmit hypertext markup language (HTML), extensible markup language (XML) or other pages to client browsers.
ID	A set of characters, usually an email address or name, that serve as a private identifying string when paired with a password.
IMAP	Internet Message Access Protocol to retrieve email messages from a server over the Internet.

Term	Definition
Internet	A worldwide electronic network supporting electronic digital data transmission, used primarily for website-user communication (i.e. the World Wide Web or www).
Internet Protocol	Specifies the format of packets and the addressing scheme
IP Address	A unique binary number used to identify devices on a TCP/IP network
ISP	Internet Service Provider – the enterprise that provides access to the Internet in your home or business
Keylogger	A technology that records consecutive keystrokes on a keyboard to capture username and password information
LAN	Local Area Network. An electronic network, typically in a single location, providing digital data communication for the local area personal computers/smartphones.
Malware	A software program designed to damage or cause unwanted actions on a computer system, including viruses, worms and Trojan horses.
MMS	Multimedia Message Service is a protocol used to send multimedia messages among mobile phones.
Modem	A device that connects data transmission from a public data network to a LAN, usually by converting analog data to digital data.
Network name	See SSID – the name of a Wi-Fi network.

Term	Definition
Network sharing	A means to share resources (e.g.files and printers) over a network.
Operating System	Software that typically is supplied with a personal computer or smartphone to enable it to operate and provide an environment for user applications. Examples are iOS for the iPhone or Mac or Windows 10 for the PC.
Packet	A small amount of digital data that contains sufficient information to allow it to be routed over a data network, such as the Internet.
Password	A set of characters that serve as a private identifying string when paired with an ID.
Phishing	A hacking method that sends emails to users that attempts to harvest personal information for theft.
POP	Post Office Protocol used to retrieve email messages from a server over the Internet.
Proxy server	A server that acts on behalf of a user. Typical proxies accept a connection from a user, make a decision as to whether the user or client IP address is permitted to use the proxy, perhaps perform additional authentication, and complete a connection a remote destination o behalf of the user.
Ransomware	A type of malware that restricts access to personal computer systems until the target pays a ransom to the malware operators to remove the restriction.

Cyber Security for Seniors
W. Glossary

Term	Definition
Rootkit	A software suite designed to aid an intruder in gaining unauthorized administrative access to a personal computer.
Router	A network-connected device that routes packets of digital data across a LAN or wide-area network (WAN)
Server	A typically-centralized computer system that sends/receives data from one or more users' personal computers/smartphones.
SFTP	Secure File Transfer Protocol is a secure version of FTP.
Short code	A 5-6 digit smartphone number for SMS texting transmissions. People use short codes to send a text message to subscribe to a mass texting campaign; for example the incoming text is: "text JOIN to 313131." "JOIN" is the keyword and 313131 is the short code.
Skimming, skimmer	A method used by scammers to capture information from a credit cardholder. An advanced approach involves using a small device called a skimmer at an ATM or other public credit card reader to steal personal information.
Smart Home	A home that has one or more LAN-networked, electronic devices able to be controlled by the home-owner.
Smart TV	A television with a supporting computer, connected to the LAN.
Smishing	The texting version of phishing.

Cyber Security for Seniors
W. Glossary

Term	Definition
SMS	Short Message Service is a protocol used to send text messages among mobile phones.
SMTP	Simple Mail Transfer **Protocol** is used for sending e-mail messages between servers; the messages can then be retrieved with an e-mail client using either POP or IMAP.
Spam	Computer-generated messages sent as unsolicited advertising
Smishing, smished	A phishing message sent via text.
Spoofing	Faking the sending address of a transmission in order to gain illegal entry into a secure system
Spyware	Software whose purpose is to monitor a personal computer user's actions (e.g. web sites visited) and report these actions to a third party, without the informed consent of that machine's owner or legitimate user
SSID	Service Set ID; the network name for a wireless local area network
SSL Certificate	Indicates minimal verification and encryption of website domain. See EV certificate.
Surveillance capitalism	Using data captured through monitoring people's online and physical world behavior for personalized marketing and advertising.
TCP/IP	Transmission Control Protocol/ Internet Protocol controls the connection of computer systems on Internet.

Term	Definition
TDMA	Time Division Multiple Access protocol is used to transmit digital data over 2G mobile phone networks.
TOR browser	Tor is an anonymity network that provides software designed to allow access of the Internet anonymously. With Tor, the user's signal is routed through a number of nodes, each of which is only aware of the IP addresses 'in front' of the node and 'behind' it. The whole path between the originating computer and the desired website remains obscured.
Trojan horse	Purposefully hidden malicious or damaging code within an authorized computer program. Unlike viruses, they do not replicate themselves, but they can be just as destructive to a single personal computer
Two-factor Authentication	In addition to authentication through an ID and password combination, a separate numeric code is sent to a secondary device and returned to provide improved security.
uBlock Origin	A free and open-source, cross-platform browser extension for content-filtering, including ad-blocking. The extension is available for several browsers: Chrome, Chromium, Edge, Firefox, Opera and Safari.
UPnP	**Universal Plug and Play (UPnP)** is a set of protocols that permit networked devices to discover each other to share data, communications, and entertainment.

Term	Definition
Virus	Software introduced into a personal computer/smartphone for destructive or mercenary purposes.
Virtual private network (VPN)	A secure private network that uses the Internet to transmit data. Using encryption and authentication, a VPN encrypts all data that pass between two Internet points, maintaining privacy and security
Vishing	The voice version of a phishing attack
Watering Hole Attack	Hackers plant malicious code on trusted websites that they hope their targets would visit. The code records visitors' confidential information to enable specific acts of espionage, theft or mayhem.
WEP	Wired Equivalent Privacy (WEP), the original Wi-Fi security (encryption) standard, now essentially replaced by WPA2 and WPA3.
Whaling	A spear-phishing technique that targets high-net-worth individuals, family offices and corporate executives
WiFi	a facility allowing personal computers, smartphones, or other devices to connect to the Internet or communicate with one another wirelessly within a particular area.
Wi-Fi Protected Access II (WPA2)	Wireless security protocol that supports 802-11i encryption standards to provide greater security.

Term	Definition
Worm	a type of malware that spreads copies of itself from personal computer to personal computer. A worm can replicate itself without any human interaction, and it does not need to attach itself to a software program in order to cause damage.
WIFI	A term for technology for radio wireless local area networking of devices.
World Wide Web	An information system on the Internet that allows documents to be connected to other documents by hypertext links, enabling the user to search for information by moving from one document to another.
WPA2, WPA3	Wi-Fi Protected Access (**WPAx**) are data encryption standards for users of computing devices equipped with wireless Internet connections.

Index

Cyber Security for Seniors
Index

Cyber Security for Seniors
Index

Made in the USA
Monee, IL
07 December 2019